Mechanics of
COMPANY
COMMAND

CPT Bryan Langley

Mechanics of Company Command

1st Edition, 1st Printing

PUBLISHED BY

MENTOR ENTERPRISES, INC.

ISBN-13: 978-1-940370-11-8

ISBN-10: 1-940370-11-6

The views expressed in this book are those of the author and do not reflect the official policy or position of the United States Army, Defense Department, or the United States Government.

DISCLAIMER

The content of this product is a compilation of information and personal experience from the author, numerous contributors and editors.

It is possible that mistakes may be found in both content and typography.

This book should and can only be used as a **guide**. Information gleaned from this product should be modified according to existing situations by seeking guidance from competent professionals including your chain of command, military lawyers, inspector generals, or other competent staff professionals.

No warranty is made or implied with regard to completeness and/or correctness, legal effect, or validity of this product in any state or jurisdiction. It is further understood that any person or entity that uses this product does so at their own risk with full knowledge that they have a legal obligation, duty, and responsibility to ensure the information they use or provide to others is in accordance with up-to-date military law, procedure, regulation, policy, and order. No part of this product shall in any way substitute for professional guidance or regulatory requirement.

CONTENTS

We've provided several documents online to help you manage your command!

View available documents at: asktop.net/mocc
Password: 88YEZX9

Any updates or corrections to this book will also be available
at the web address listed above.

INTRODUCTION
LEADERSHIP VS. MANAGEMENT

This book is not about leadership. Leadership involves making decisions based on your priorities. It includes adapting to different environments, adjusting practices to current or future trends, and is centered on motivating people to follow your directives in order to achieve a desired outcome.

Unfortunately, I can't tell you how to lead your company. No one can, because no one else knows your operational environment, your priorities, or the desired end state for your company.[1]

So what is this book about if it's not about leadership? It is about management. What's our definition of management? For the purpose of this book we define management as efficiently completing required tasks assigned by a higher echelon. It's not about adjusting dynamically to a changing environment—it's about achieving the greatest performance in a static environment. To the extent that it involves change, it's evolutionary rather than revolutionary—attacked in incremental steps rather than quantum leaps—and focused on achieving peak efficiency. Management is about controlling systems to generate measurable, quantitative, consistently effective performance with predictable regularity.

> Management is about controlling systems to generate measurable, quantitative, consistently effective performance with predictable regularity.

The Army places enormous value on leadership. Unfortunately, leadership experience, leadership qualities, and leadership values are hard to

---

[1] For the sake of simplicity, this term "company" also includes troops, batteries, and detachments.

teach, difficult to measure, and predominately acquired through years of experience and exposure to Army culture.

By comparison, the Army places little value on company management. This is surprising, given the need for strong managers and organizers at the company level, and how easily its systematic requirements can be taught. Given the Army's bureaucratic, hierarchical structures and their static, regular requirements, company commanders could benefit from instruction on a set of managerial best practices— what needs to be done and who best to do it.

This is not to denigrate leadership. When it comes to company command, you will need leadership abilities as well as management skills. Your leadership will be tested when you must discipline a Soldier for under-age drinking—will you "throw the book" at them, or consider mitigating circumstances? But managerial competency is needed to balance your unit's competing personnel development, training, administrative, supply, operational, disciplinary, family readiness, maintenance, and substance abuse prevention requirements.

Fortunately, the Army has already decided the "right" things you must do. The hard part is figuring out how to do them all effectively.

This book attempts to help company grade officers by filling in the experience gap between leadership and management through best practices, experience, and lessons learned.

Good luck.

PART I: BEFORE TAKING COMMAND

MANAGEMENT BASICS

"Efficiency is doing things right; effectiveness is doing the right things."
—*Peter Drucker*

Whether you wish to pursue a career with the Army or eventually move to the private sector, knowledge of basic management principles will help in understanding how things work in the real world. Whether in the Army or the civilian world, employees behave the same way.

In the Army, following the principles of management will improve your ability to "Exercise Mission Command" through improved "science of control."[1] (See chart on next page). The commander who can quickly establish and effectively utilize their Mission Command Systems gains a clear advantage in directing unit operations.

Your ability to manage—defined as the effective utilization of personnel and equipment toward a common objective, guided by processes and procedures—will be evaluated in large part by your ability to direct people. So let's start with some key terms and concepts.

---

[1] ADP 6-0 Figure 1, May 2014

Unified Land Operations

How the Army seizes, retains, and exploits the initiative to gain and maintain a position of relative advantage in sustained land operations through simultaneous offensive, defensive, and stability operations in order to prevent or deter conflict, prevail in war, and create the conditions for favorable conflict resolution.

 One of the foundations is...

Nature of Operations

Military operations are human endeavors.

They are contests of wills characterized by continuous and mutual adaptation by all participants.

Army forces conduct operations in complex, ever-changing, and uncertain operational environments.

To account for this, the Army exercises...

Mission Command Philosophy

Exercise of authority and direction by the commander using mission orders to enable disciplined initiative within the commander's intent to empower agile and adaptive leaders in the conduct of unified land operations.

Guided by the principles of...

- Build cohesive teams through mutual trust
- Create shared understanding
- Provide a clear commander's intent
- Exercise disciplined initiative
- Use mission orders
- Accept prudent risk

The principles of mission command assist commanders and staff in blending the **art of command** *with the* **science of control.**

Executed through the...

Mission Command Warfighting Function

The related tasks and systems that develop and integrate those activities enabling a commander to balance the art of command and the science of control in order to integrate the other warfighting functions.

A series of mutually supported tasks ..

Commander Tasks:
- Drive the operations process through the activities of understand, visualize, describe, direct, lead, and assess
- Develop teams, both within their own organizations and with unified action partners
- Inform and influence audiences, inside and outside their organizations

Leads

Supports

Staff Tasks:
- Conduct the operations process (plan, prepare, execute, and assess)
- Conduct knowledge management and information management
- Synchronize information-related capabilities
- Conduct cyber electromagnetic activities

Additional Tasks:
- Conduct military deception
- Conduct civil affairs operations
- Conduct airspace control
- Install, operate, and maintain the network
- Conduct information protection

Enabled by a system...

Mission Command System:
- **Personnel**
- **Networks**
- **Information systems**
- **Processes and procedures**
- **Facilities and equipment**

Together, the mission command philosophy and warfighting function guide, integrate, and synchronize Army forces throughout the conduct of unified land operations.

Delegation

Clearly, no commander can do everything alone—there simply aren't enough hours in the day. In order to complete all required tasks (and successfully train personnel in their jobs) a commander needs to delegate work to subordinates.

Delegation not only shares the workload across a team of individuals, but also provides a shared sense of purpose. Soldiers volunteer for the military not because they want to make an easy paycheck, but because they want to be of service. Delegation provides this , but it requires clear communication to assign it.

Management by Objective

Most people learn their jobs by "office osmosis." Imagine this situation. You've just arrived at your new battalion and are meeting with the boss for your initial counseling. Yet instead of learning about your duties and responsibilities on staff, they start with this:

"I can't really say what your job will be," they say, "but here's what I need help with right now." As you complete that task, you're given another, then another, until over time you form a general idea what your role is. No one ever clearly spells out what your left and right limits are—your boss is too busy doing their job to explain what yours is—but eventually you find a role for yourself in the office and become more productive.

Meanwhile, you learn who the strong performers are in the office, and who's been sidelined. You're all drawing the same paycheck, but for whatever reason some people have the boss's trust and work harder and while others seem to skate by unchallenged.

It happens all the time, but this is the exact opposite of how things are supposed to work. Instead of having to muddle through your first couple weeks, you should be able to move into a new position and know not only what your job responsibilities, but also your rater's and your senior rater's. You, as a subordinate, should be able to see how you fit into the larger picture so you can then contribute to that shared goal. That way, at the end of your rating period, your performance can be compared against a common standard of performance for your position and be evaluated objectively.

The private sector calls this management by objective, and—officially, at least—it's the Army's principal management technique. As explained in AR 623-3, an initial counseling conducted within the first 30 days "aids in developing a duty description for the Soldier and identifying major performance objectives to accomplish during the rating period."[2] Through follow-up counselings, the rated soldier and rater "discuss and document significant contributions" and "performance accomplishments" so that rated soldiers understand how their performance measures up with those initial goals.[3]

Management by objective is designed to help subordinates understand how their jobs contribute to mission success. As a commander, the effectiveness of your organization depends on being able to—as ADP 6-0 Figure 1 shows—communicate your intent to create a shared understanding. There's no better way to provide newly arriving subordinates with your vision for the unit than by a good initial counseling.

Elements of Control

While delegation is necessary, a commander cannot simply delegate tasks and expect fully effective results simply by fiat. Successful management controls align the following five elements in the same way that a boxer aligns the entire body for a punch:

---

[2] AR 623-1 §1-8e, 3 April 2014
[3] DA PAM 623-3 §2-1b(2)(b), 31 March 2014

A boxer aligns their legs, hips, shoulder, elbow, wrist, and striking surface to put the maximum amount of force into a punch. Any missing element results in a sub-optimal strike.

1. Responsibility
2. Visibility
3. Capability
4. Authority
5. Accountability

Responsibility

While commanders may delegate tasks, they still remain responsible for the tasks themselves. Delegation does not absolve commanders of their own duties. If your boss gives you a task, you can delegate it to a lieutenant. However, if they fail, your boss will not want to hear any excuses—you remain responsible. As any battalion commander will be quick to tell you, if they wanted to manage lieutenants, they wouldn't need you.

> *"Commanders are responsible for everything their command does or fails to do."—Army Regulation 600-20 §2-1b, 6 November 2014*

The same goes for you, too. You have lieutenants to whom you assign responsibilities, and they should feel free to pass them on, too. But they too should understand that while they may delegate, the ultimate responsibility to complete the tasks that you've assigned remains with with them.

Visibility

Stepping on a scale. Plotting your location. Checking the stopwatch. Before you can make any progress on a project—whether it's losing weight, conducting land navigation, or improving your run time—you first have to know where you're at. After all, if you don't know what the problem is, how can you fix it? Gaining visibility is about understanding what the problem is in order to correct it.

> *"Furious activity is no substitute for understanding."—H.H. Williams*[4]

Most meetings at the battalion level and higher are about providing visibility, which is critical to monitoring progress and measuring success. Weekly significant action (SIGACT) presentations, quarterly training briefs, and command and staff meetings are all about gaining, sharing, and maintaining organizational visibility. If you've ever been corrected for "making sausage" (working out details) in a meeting, you've learned that the meeting's sole purpose is to brief the boss, i.e. provide visibility.

Higher echelons need visibility to keep the pulse of their organizations, but it's also critical for subordinates to understand the current status within their areas of responsibility. In the days before smartphones enabled quick access to digital information, platoon leaders kept visibility on their soldiers' readiness by maintaining thick binders filled with scorecards and training certificates.

These days, access to online databases have replaced binders as the most efficient way to monitor readiness, allowing First Sergeants to use MEDPROS access to see if soldiers are current on their immunizations. The purpose is the same—to identify and proactively correct issues before someone else tells you to.

As company commander, you should have access to all the systems your subordinates use, not only to grant access, but also to keep watch on how well people are going their jobs. A commander should never rely exclusively on others to provide visibility on unit functions.

---

[4] http://www.quotationspage.com/quotes/H._H._Williams/

Capability

Unlike in the private sector, unit commanders do not set salaries or select human resources. The skill set with which a soldier comes to the unit is—for the most part—beyond the command team's control. However, by identifying and developing the right people for the right tasks, mission accomplishment becomes much easier.

How do you know who's the most capable person for any task? It will be the one with the **Time**, **Training**, and **Tenacity** to handle the job.

First, does the solder have the time to dedicate to this task? Obviously, the number of other tasks a person must complete will affect the amount of time any one person can dedicate to something else. For this reason, it's often better to choose a platoon leader for a commander's inquiry rather than your executive officer.

Second, have they been trained in that function? Some additional duties, such as Unit Movement Officer, require a two-week training course. Others, like Unit Prevention Leader or Sexual Harassment/Assault Response Program (SHARP) coordinator, require not only training but an unblemished record. Rather than train a new person, you may be better off picking someone for the task who's already trained.

> *"Civilization is one long, anxious search for just such individuals."*
> —Elbert Hubbard

Finally, do they have the mental tenacity to push through the inevitable obstacles that will occur? In "A Letter to Garcia," you see an example of this.[5] Employers have long bemoaned the lack of capable people who can obey instructions without needless questions (like "Why do *I* have to do this?"), work diligently without supervision, and complete assignments on time. They want people who understand the big picture, show initiative, and do the right thing without being told.

---

[5] "A Letter to Garcia," Elbert Hubbard, 1899

More than any other characteristic, tenacity will be the hallmark of your most capable people.

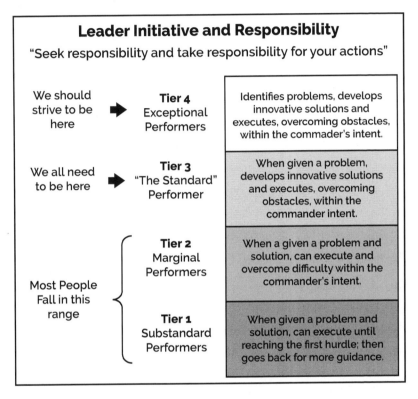

Leader Initiative and Responsibility
"Seek responsibility and take responsibility for your actions"

We should strive to be here ➡	**Tier 4** Exceptional Performers	Identifies problems, develops innovative solutions and executes, overcoming obstacles, within the commader's intent.
We all need to be here ➡	**Tier 3** "The Standard" Performer	When given a problem, develops innovative solutions and executes, overcoming obstacles, within the commander intent.
Most People Fall in this range	**Tier 2** Marginal Performers	When a given a problem and solution, can execute and overcome difficulty within the commander's intent.
	Tier 1 Substandard Performers	When given a problem and solution, can execute until reaching the first hurdle; then goes back for more guidance.

Authority

There are two kinds of authority: the kind you explicitly grant, and the kind that people assume for themselves through initiative. Neither is necessarily better, but your subordinates need a measure of authority to direct resources, and they need to know what you're comfortable with.

Some leaders prefer to have tighter control over their organizations in order to minimize waste—either of time, money, or effort. In these situations, the proverbial left and right limits of the firing lanes are tighter. Others prefer to widen the lane and assume a greater amount of risk in order to empower their subordinates.

> *"If your subordinates are not making an occasional mistake or two, it's a sure sign they're playing it too safe."—Tom Peters*

This quote makes underwriting a mistake sound fairly simple. Well, consider this story. One day, the commanding general at Fort Hood received a picture attached to an email of a Humvee parked at a local fast food restaurant, with the bumper numbers in plain view to identify exactly which company it belonged to. As you can imagine, the downline chain of command sprang into action to identify and discipline those responsible for this embarrassing event.

Yet upon further examination, a number of facts came to light:

- The vehicle, as shown in the picture, was properly chock-blocked, with the drip pan underneath.

- The vehicle was properly dispatched for the off-post activity and signed by the right authority.

- The driver and truck commander (TC) had just completed an off-post mission they had been properly ordered to perform.

- The TC, a sergeant, was concerned that he was not able to get the soldier back to post in time for lunch at the dining facility. Rather than have his soldier miss a meal, he treated the soldier.

Given this information, how would you handle this situation if you were the unit commander? What if this was the "occasional mistake" you had to deal with? Would you appease your chain of command and put the sergeant up for disciplinary action, or would you issue a simple correction?

Regardless of the extent to which you grant authority to your subordinates, it's important to be consistent. There are few better ways to kill someone's enthusiasm than by chewing out someone who made a mistake when trying to act in your best interests.

You will get bad news one day, but try not to react to first reports. Odds are, it's either incomplete or simply incorrect. So take a deep breath and be calm, or next time someone might not even tell you at all.

Accountability

Accountability closes the loop on management controls. It's the follow up on a task you've assigned, and can take the form of a written report (as in an investigation), a regular brief, or an informal hallway update. For subordinates, the expected measure of accountability ensures they accomplish their duties in a timely manner.

Accountability doesn't necessarily have to happen at the end of a task—commanders often ask for situation reports (SITREPs) throughout major projects. These SITREPs act as a quality control mechanism to check on progress and make sure things are happening according to schedule.

"Men do well only what their leader checks."—GEN Bruce Clarke

Yet SITREPs, while convenient, are not the most effective tools to enforce accountability in the organization. Rather than posting up behind the desk and waiting for a report to come in, "management by wandering around" is far more effective. Personally checking on events conveys the value you place on the unit's activities, and the random conversations you have with people will not only lift morale and provide a sense of organizational purpose, will allow people to ask questions they wouldn't ask otherwise.

This may seem odd, but there are many reasons people simply *will not seek you out.* They may assume you are too busy to answer their question, they're afraid of their NCOs criticizing them for not taking things through the chain of command, or they're too busy themselves to leave their work station. However, by visiting people at their place of duty, where they most feel comfortable, you can de-conflict a number of issues that—singularly—you would not otherwise have time for. This also helps to decrease "power distance"—the barriers to communication that inevitably result from the hierarchical way the Army is structured. You, after all, are *The Commander.*

So while you may want to have everyone regularly report to you just in time for the battalion commander's command and staff meeting, management by wandering around remains the most effective, and least confrontational, method to get accountability on people's projects.

Regulations, Policies, and Customs

What role should regulations play in Army culture? Are they more important than how you've always done things, or less? It may seem obvious, but the Army's regulations are in the most basic sense requirements—there is nothing optional about them. Nevertheless, you are going to find references to regulations throughout this book that your unit doesn't follow simply because they are not enforced.

One might blame that fact on the nearly incessant mission demands of the past two decades, but if we consider ourselves *professionals* then regulations are the standards we *must* follow. They cannot be optional. As a company grade officer, you take unnecessary risk upon yourself when you ignore regulation for expediency.

Below regulations, the Army has policies. Policies are local in nature, and allow each layer of command to add additional requirements to existing regulations. However, they cannot negate regulatory requirements.

Customs, traditions, and common practices have no standing in the Army's structure. They are unit-specific ways of doing things that vary from place to place. Interestingly, most people (not just soldiers) will default to these as their guiding principles, and will only alter behavior when change is forced on them.

If you find someone who both knows the regulation and advocates the Army's interests by holding to them, you've found a rare gem indeed. This person is a true Army professional — they know regulations and policies, look for best practices, and change their organization to meet the demands of relevant regulations and policies.

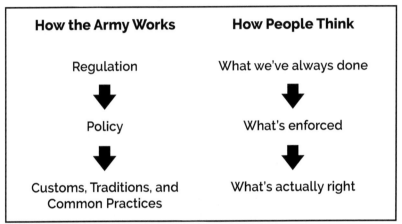

How the Army Works	How People Think
Regulation	What we've always done
⬇	⬇
Policy	What's enforced
⬇	⬇
Customs, Traditions, and Common Practices	What's actually right

Conclusion

From this chapter you've learned the basics of management as they apply to Army's science of control. You must know what needs to be done according to relevant regulations and local policies. You must assign responsibility for these tasks and train capable people to handle them. You must give them visibility to understand where the problems are, and grant them authority to deal with roadblocks. And finally, your must establish a way to track progress.

It sounds good in theory, but to put it into effect, you'll first need to get a command. So let's look at some ways to prepare for command.

2

FINDING A COMMAND

> *"It is commonplace for leaders to call a company commander's job the hardest job in the Army." —MG (Ret.) John G. Meyer*

So You Want a Command?

Command is not for everyone. It requires a dedication to soldiers' welfare that is unparalleled in the civilian world, with little chance of immediate reward and a very real risk of failure. To test the motives of potential commanders, GEN Bruce Clarke offered a series of questions in 1957 that are still relevant today:

> We hear many officers say, "I'd do anything to get a command." If you are one of these, do you really mean it? Are you suited for command? Have you really considered what having a command entails? What are your answers to the following questions?

- Are you willing to devote all hours of the day and night, seven days a week, to a command?

- Is your wife willing to do likewise when needed in order to make a happy "Army community" in your unit area?

- Is your family willing to be secondary, if necessary, to the "Company," "Battalion," "Group," "Regiment," "Combat Command," "Brigade," or "Division"?

- Are you willing to learn, teach, stress and live with the "basic fundamentals" necessary to make your unit good and still believe that your great talents for "bigger things" are not being wasted?

- Do you like to be with young people? Can you live with their energy, points of view, and the problems they create?

- Are you willing to take the hard knocks that come from carrying responsibility for the failure of your subordinates?

- Can you juggle, at the same time, all the balls of training, maintenance, tests, administration, inspections, communications, messes, supply, athletics, marksmanship, discipline, public relations, without dropping any of them?

- Are you able to do many things "concurrently," or are you a "conservative" doer? Can you manage a complex job?

- Can you receive and carry out orders? Are you a good "follower" as well as a "leader"?

- Can you stand tough competitions from like units in your outfit and still retain a spirit of cooperation and teamwork with them?

- Are you physically and emotionally fit to carry the load?

- Do you have the courage to make and stand by tough decisions?

- Are you and your family willing to "live in goldfish bowl" where your actions are closely observed by both subordinates and superiors?

- Are you still enthusiastic and cheerful when confronted with seemingly impossible tasks to performed with inadequate means?

- Are you willing to take responsibility yourself when things go wrong in your unit and correct a bad situation rather than blame it on the staff or a higher headquarters or a subordinate?

- Are you willing to do your best with "what you have" even though it apparently is inadequate?

- Are you confident you can produce a superior unit with the ordinary run of manpower? Can you inspire personnel to produce outstanding accomplishment?

- Are you willing to take a chance on being relived for attaining only mediocre results?

- Do you really want "command" or do you just want "to get command on your record"?

If your answers to these questions are "Yes," you should fight to get a command. And, if you hear an officer say "I want a command," you should confront him with these questions. If his answers are "Yes," he is undoubtedly sincere and you should make every effort to see that he gets a command. No assignment will ever give greater satisfaction or enable an officer to contribute more to the Army and our Country.

Many officers seek command because it is their branch's only key developmental (KD) billet, but that is not the case for every branch. Military Intelligence, Signal, and Adjutant General have so few command opportunities that being a battalion level primary staff OIC is accepted as KD.

In addition, several functional areas do not require branch qualification in order to transfer, including Telecommunications System Engineer (FA24), Electronic Warfare (FA29), and Information Systems Management (FA53)[1]

Yet for most branches, the one key developmental billet is company command, and the selection boards for major look more favorably on files that include successful company command time. For selection as a battalion commander, it is almost certainly a requirement.

Your professional timeline should determine how picky you are about the companies you choose to interview for. If you are late to command for your year group, you should interview for every opportunity possible. If you are fairly early, you can afford to be more selective.

Yet one mistake you should never make is to turn down a command offer after you've interviewed for it. Even if it's not your first choice, there's no such thing as a "better offer." This is the Army, and "Self-Sacrifice" is the Army Value at work here.

Consider this perspective: anyone who is offered command will have been selected from a pool of undoubtedly well qualified captains to lead Soldiers who have volunteered for service in the United States Army. Is any of us so prized an officer that we can afford to dismiss a colonel's command offer, thinking another will beg us to join their team instead?

It is more likely that your offer has been negotiated by your superiors so there is no hint of conflict at that level. So don't turn down any offer of command.

---

[1] FY2016 First Quarter VTIP
https://www.hrc.army.mil/Milper/PrintPreview.aspx?MILPERID=15-259

Know the System

Selection for command works differently from place to place, depending on local division or brigade level policies. One unit may use an order of merit list based on year group, a second may do assessment boards, while a third allows battalion commanders to choose independently. Regardless, selection for company command is one of the few times in an officer's career that requires applying and interviewing for a position.

Things begin soon after you arrive at your duty station following your captain's career course. When you introduce yourself to your battalion commander, you need to mention that you are interested in taking a command. You must also ask two questions: 1.) How company commanders are selected, and 2.) How the brigade commander feels about captains interviewing outside the brigade. If the division-level headquarters maintains an order of merit list, talk to your battalion S-1 to make sure you're on it.

Understanding the brigade commander's view on interviewing outside the organization is important because they hold the sole authority to release officers, and some view interviewing outside the organization too quickly as disloyalty.

Once you have permission, you can begin to look at surrounding brigades to see when openings will become available. For example, every combat aviation battalion has a forward support company with a logistician (90A) commander billet, even though the MTOE has no authorization for a logistician staff officer. That battalion commander has no choice but to bring someone in from outside their organization, and will definitely be interested in widening their selection pool.

Similarly, be on the lookout for installation and higher echelon headquarters commands. These branch immaterial opportunities are still branch qualifying, viable alternatives to the typical line companies.

To find out which organizations on your installation have what positions, take the time to look up the MTOE for every unit in your area on FMSWeb[2]. Not only will it show what positions are available, but you can see what the field of potential competition is.

> "It's not the will to win that matters—everyone has that. It's the will to prepare to win that matters."—Paul "Bear" Bryant

Prepare for the Interview

When a position becomes available, you'll receive an email notification inviting you to apply and listing what documents you need to submit (typically an ORB, your last several OERs, a five year plan, and a personal biography). Submit your packet promptly and you'll be contacted to set up an appointment. If you haven't heard anything after a few days, contact the unit's S1 to confirm they received your packet.

Before you meet with your prospective boss,

1. **Research the unit.** Understand what its mission is, what the MTOE looks like, and if there is an associated Table of Distribution and Allowance (TDA). Understand the background of the person interviewing you, their professional background, and how long they have been in command (if it's been almost two years, you may be working for their successor).

2. **Review common interview questions.** What goals do you have for yourself? How do you evaluate success? What motivates you?

---

[2] FMSWeb
https://fmsweb.army.mil/unprotected/splash/

These kinds of questions help your future boss understand what kind of leader you will be. Having clear, concise, and relevant answers will help distinguish you from other candidates. Review this list of 150 interview questions[3]; the more questions for which you can provide well-rehearsed one-minute answers, the better prepared you will be.

3. **Reflect on what you've seen.** Draw on your experiences in the Army, whether good or bad, to form your own opinions about what is important. What does "right" look like? What would you have done differently if you'd been in charge? Speak honestly, but don't denigrate your previous bosses—after all, this may be your future boss you're talking to.

During the Interview

As you go to your interview, be sure to do the following:

1. **Dress for success.** Most interviews are in the Army Combat Uniform, though having your Army Service Uniform ready and available is a good practice. Make sure your uniform presents a neat and orderly appearance in accordance with Army Regulation 670-1, and be sure to wear the newest authorized camouflage pattern. Brush your teeth or eat a mint beforehand, and by all means do NOT use tobacco products. Also, keep a notepad in one of your pockets to take notes.

2. **Arrive early.** Plan to get there 10-15 minutes before your appointment. If you have to drive, make sure you've reconned the route, or have allotted plenty of time for unforeseen traffic problems.

3. **Turn off all electronic devices.** Unless your spouse is about to give birth, the interview is the only thing you should care about.

4. **Be courteous to everyone.** From your prospective boss to the lowest private (who may be the boss's driver), your interactions

---

[3] http://www.quintcareers.com/interview_question_database/interview_questions.html

will form first impressions that will last. Even if you don't get the position you're interviewing for right then, your name may come up later if you've left a good impression.

5. **Be confident, authentic, and concise.** Being prepared will help you show confidence. Reflecting on your experiences will help your responses feel genuine. Rehearsing interview questions will help keep your responses short and focused.

6. **Avoid bad habits.** Avoid unnecessary slang, crude language, and risqué jokes—remember that the Army is a profession of arms, and you are its representative. Poor body language and speaking manners will not instill confidence in the interviewer that you can lead a company.

7. **Prepare thoughtful questions.** What are the boss's priorities? What direction do they want to take the unit in? How is performance measured? What are the boss's professional strengths and weaknesses? At the end of the interview, you may have the chance to ask these kinds of questions. If the best way to judge a person's intelligence is by the *questions* they ask, you should expect your interpersonal skills will be gauged even more by what you ask than how you answer.

8. **Express thanks.** At the end of the interview, be sure to express your gratitude. Also, send a written note as soon as possible. (If necessary, get the address while you're at the location, write it out in the car, and send it immediately.) Send an email after one week to make sure it got there. Such actions will leave a positive impression.

9. **Leave a "Pick Me" binder and follow up.** Battalion commanders may speak with dozens of officers to fill a position. As the interview ends, leave a tabbed binder of the application materials mentioned above to help your interviewer remember you. If you haven't heard anything within a week, contact the S1 and ask if a decision has been made.[4]

---

[4] Adapted from Dr. Randall S. Hansen's ten tips for job seekers. http://www.quintcareers.com/job_interview_tips.html

Avoid unnecessary slang, crude language, and riskqué jokes—remember that the Army is a profession of arms, and you are its representative.

Other Tips

Interviewing can be a stressful process. As you prepare for your command interviews, bear in mind there are certain things you can control, and others you can't.

Things You Can't Control

1. **Past jobs.** You may not have had all the "right" jobs, or had as much experience at the battalion/brigade level as you'd like, but don't let that hold you back. Higher level commanders are just as interested—if not more—in your judgment and leadership qualities as in your job experiences.

2. **Your interviewer.** You can't change what they're looking for in a company commander, what their priorities are, or what their organization needs. While battalion commanders are always looking for the best qualified person, they are also looking for the right "fit" for the unit. There are a number of factors that go into choosing a company commander. Sometimes, they may not even be the one who makes the final decision—it may be the brigade commander—so don't take the inevitable setbacks personally. Your attitude, tenacity, tone, and sincerity matter, but you'll never know how your interviewer prioritizes those values.

3. **External factors.** Be aware that you can't control your place in the order of merit, the character of the organization, or how many other candidates there are. Just because you haven't been selected yet doesn't mean you won't be.

Things Under Your Control

1. **Attitude.** Whether you're on your first interview or your tenth, go in with the understanding that command is a privilege, not an entitlement. Consider it an honor to even be a candidate.

2. **Preparedness.** Genuine, "authentic leadership" comes from your own experiences.[5] Look back on what you learned in your previous positions, including any investigations you've done, ethical dilemmas you faced, and problems you solved. What have you seen that you didn't like, or would have done differently? How has this affected your perspective of command? Have these stories fresh in your mind so you can draw on them during the interview, and have your command philosophy on hand.

3. **Expectations.** Very few officers get their first choice of command. Don't try to game the system by picking and choosing which companies you will or won't interview for—any command position is a command position. Interview for every one you can—if nothing else, it's a learning experience that will help you improve in the next interview.

4. **Refining your skills.** If you've been interviewing for a year and yet you still haven't gotten an offer, you likely have a professional issue. Have you pursued schools and experience from various positions? Solicit input from your rater and senior rater how you can improve your candidacy, and ask those you've worked with to take part in an MSAF 360. MSAF 360 mentors are available as on request to discuss the results with you as a neutral party.

---

[5] "Discovering Your Authentic Leadership," Bill George et al, Harvard Business Review, May 2009

War Stories

Consider these five experiences in interviewing for a command:

1. Thirty candidates interviewed for a headquarters company in a logistics battalion. Only five of them left a "Pick Me" book to help the interviewer recall what each person was like. The one selected for command came from the group of five.

2. One battalion commander had narrowed the field of candidates down to two. The tiebreaker question was, "What would you do in the first 90 days?" While one captain fumbled around, the other answered they would do an assessment and report back to the BC with what they found. The second captain got the job.

3. An aviation commander was concerned about severe disciplinary problems in their battalion. Their make-it-or-break-it question involved how the candidate would administer UCMJ actions. One successful candidate drew on their experience as a summary court martial officer to underscore the importance of being both fair and firm.

4. An air defense artillery commander was looking for a captain to lead the maintenance company. Not wanting to do a lengthy search, he heavily weighted the personal recommendations of his subordinates. The decision followed quickly.

5. When asked, "What direction will you take the company?" two candidates offered distinctly different views of what the company should train on. While both candidates provided perfectly sound visions for the unit, the battalion commander went with the captain whose goals coincided with their own.

6. One captain interviewed for a command position after only two months of battalion staff experience. Though they didn't get that position, they left such a good impression that the same battalion commander remembered them months later and selected them for the next company that opened up.

In the end, being prepared does not guarantee you a position. Nevertheless, you improve your chances by offering well-practiced, genuine, concise responses in a professional manner.

Conclusion

"If at first you don't succeed, try, try again." "Practice makes perfect." They sound trite, but interviewing really is a skill, and this process won't last forever. No matter what, relax. At least you're still getting a paycheck—most college graduates don't have that going for them while they're interviewing.

Interview Question Answering Tactics

This section lists common questions and some recommended answering tactics.

1. **Tell me about yourself.**
   Focus on your accomplishments, skills set, and responsibilities. Use words like "we" and "team," to show how you work with others. Don't talk about your hobbies and pets.

2. **What are your goals?**
   Look to match the unit's mission and needs. Are you trying to broaden your experience or specialize in a particular area? Don't simply talk about getting a KD billet.

3. **Does your current battalion commander know you're looking?**
   A truthful "yes" is the right answer.

4. **What can you contribute?**
   Supply discipline is in big demand, but look to match the unit's mission. Talking about running convoys doesn't tend to impress aviation maintenance people.

5. **Have you ever faced an ethical dilemma? How'd you solve it?**
Focus on how you enforced standards or addressed a SHARP or EO related issue, and talk about how your decision led to the long term health of the unit rather than short term interests.

6. **How do you gauge training effectiveness?**
Answers may be simple—DTMS is the "acid test" because it measures 1.) training completion, and 2.) administrative competence.

7. **What is the role of the 1SG?**
Are they your battle buddy, senior advisor, or primary executor? While you must respect their experience, remember that you must still answer to the battalion commander.

8. **What are your long term goals for the company?**
Focus on a new direction you can take the unit. Have sergeant's time training or physical training been weak? What issues have you seen from your time on staff? Units typically have similar problems across brigades.

9. **Where does SHARP fit in with your priorities?**
Soldiers deserve to be treated with dignity; it is everyone's job to promote an atmosphere that reflects the Army Value of Respect, regardless of whether it's up, down, or across the chain of command.

3

PREPARING FOR COMMAND

"There is no type of human endeavor where it is so important that the leader understand all phases of his job as that of the profession of arms."
–MG James C. Fry

Congratulations! You've been offered command of a company-level unit in the United States Army. Given the authority and responsibility with which you'll soon be entrusted, it is a distinct privilege to have been selected for this position. As a commander, you owe it to yourself and your Soldiers to be as prepared as possible, and the first steps to a successful command begin long before the change of command ceremony.

Schedule the Company Commander/First Sergeant's Course

To enroll in your installation's Company Commander/First Sergeant Course (CC/FSC), contact your unit's schools NCO. The Army requires that all designated company commanders and first sergeants attend the Pre-Command Course prior to assuming duties. [1] Part of being an effective command team is knowing the relevant programs, policies, procedures, and command team responsibilities from the start.

---

[1] AR 350-1 §3-39a(1), 19 August 2014

As a commander, it's particularly important to attend the CC/FSC before even beginning the change of command inventory. The opportunity to learn from other attendees' experiences will allow you to avoid the same pitfalls that incoming commanders invariably face. If you can't, you'll be at a disadvantage. Incoming commanders who don't understand what right looks like before they begin will not even realize they've made a mistake until long afterward, when it's nearly impossible to correct.

Perform Due Diligence

In the private sector, buyers perform "due diligence" to find out what a purchase is truly worth before making a final offer. Similarly, you must do your own due diligence to understand your company's strengths and weaknesses. To get an accurate picture, you'll need to speak with an entire network of people—other commanders, installation organizations, and key individuals—all with their own perspectives.

You'll have met with the battalion commander for the job interview, but you should speak with the battalion sergeant major and the battalion executive officer as well. Some questions to ask are:

- What will the battalion commander (BC) want from me in the first 90 days?

- What aspects of leadership are most important to the BC?

- Do you have any recommendations before I take command?

- What are the unit's current strengths and weaknesses?

Questions you can ask the inspector general's office, the judge advocate general's office, and the provost marshal are:

- What do you think company commanders should know before they take command?

- What services do you offer commanders and who's the best person to contact?

- What do the best companies do that I should imitate?

- What kinds of issues do you help company commanders with?

The goal is to find out what responsibilities you have to these organizations, and who you can go to when you have a problem. And don't neglect the battalion staff sections—they will have recurring requirements that you should be aware of, too.

Meet the First Sergeant

You've probably heard it before: "The company commander **commands** the unit, and the first sergeant **runs** it."[2] Your relationship with the first sergeant will be the most important one in the company, so it's important that you operate from the "same page." Take the time to sit down with the first sergeant to understand who they are and what they bring to the table. These are some questions to ask:

- What jobs have you had in the Army?

- What experience in your career are you proudest of?

- What do you see as the First Sergeant's role in a company?

- What's your command philosophy?

- What are the executive officer's strengths and weaknesses?

- What goals should we have for the unit?

- What are your expectations of me?

By the end of the conversation, you should know about their knowledge, skills, and abilities, as well as where they'd like to take the company. The first sergeant will be your primary advisor and power partner, so it's

---

[2] Company Command The Bottom Line, p.30.

important to work together. If you can manage this, you'll double your productivity. However, if you fight each other, your soldiers will learn to play one off against the other and you'll be counterproductive.

Meet the Executive Officer

If the first sergeant **runs** the company, the executive officer **administers** it. Your relationship with the executive officer will be the second-most important in your company. Your XO's job will be to handle the day to day paperwork, lead the headquarters platoon, and stand in your place when you are on leave. You might also want to put them in charge of communicating with the platoon leaders.

As your most experienced lieutenant, your XO will have some valid opinions, too. Some questions to ask include:

- What's been your experience in the military so far?

- What are your current responsibilities?

- What do you like most about your job?

- What is the company good at? Where does it need to improve?

- Who do you supervise and what are their strengths?

By the end of this conversation, you should understand what motivates your executive officer, what kinds of tasks they can handle, and how well they know their subordinates' jobs. This will be key in deciding what kinds of tasks you can delegate.

Finalize Your Command Philosophy

Private sector organizations have mission statements to spell out their highest goals; your command philosophy should do the same for your organization by describing your vision and explaining your priorities. Once you've heard from various interested parties, finish writing yours. It can be a simple one that spells out your top three priorities, or one that's far more in depth.[3]

> *"Think like a wise man but communicate in the language of the people."*
> —*William Butler Yeats*

If you want to draw up something comprehensive, you can treat it like an initial counseling for the company. Some of the areas you might like to address are:

- The unit's purpose

- Goals for collective training

- Expectations of on and off duty conduct

- Regular reporting requirements (if you want to do a "Play of the Week" award)

- Unit standards for training, maintenance, physical fitness, and safety

- Expectations for monthly counseling statements

- How to treat soldiers' educational opportunities

- Standards for reenlistment and awards

- Role of the Family Readiness Group

- Your critical information requirements (when you need to get a phone call)

- How to handle VIP visits

---

[3] Part-Time-Commander.com posted one that focused on training, leader development, and unit readiness: http://www.part-time-commander.com/sample-company-commander-command-philosophy/

When finalizing your command philosophy, you should consider your audience, and remember to leave room for individuals' initial counseling statements. Also, there are some areas that you won't need to address in a command philosophy. Equal opportunity, hazing, bullying, and sexual harassment/sexual assault require separate policy letters.

Stamps, Logos, Emblems, Mottos, and Coins

To save time on periodic reports, you should get a signature block stamp. It should follow this format:[4]

T.R. TRAVIS	FIRST NAME LAST NAME
Captain, IN	Rank [spelled out], Branch initials
Commanding	Commanding

The unit's logo is its name; the emblem is the picture that goes with the logo; the motto is what the formation says when it comes to attention. If you and your first sergeant want to change any of these, the upcoming change of command is the best time. Be careful, though—units with strong traditions may resist a logo change. Updating the emblem or changing the motto is less controversial.

Of course, you should check with higher before changing any of them. Typically, divisional units won't allow you to change your logo. Some units require that the logo begin with the same first letter as the company (e.g. Bravo Company "Bulldogs"). Non-divisional units and battalions with numbered companies seem more flexible.

Company coins are useful for recognizing soldier accomplishments in that middle ground between a hearty handshake and an Army Achievement Award. Company coins are usually not Army funded, but sourcing them with your own money allows you to put your name on them and give them to whomever you want. You'll have to pay a fixed fee

[4] See AR 25-50 §6-4 and Figure D-5, 17 May 2013

for the mold and a variable cost depending on the type and number of coins you order.

Coin companies offer a wide variety of designs, including bottle cap openers and irregular shapes. For a typical company, 100 coins should be enough to last you 18 months. Just remember to get permission from higher before you put in an order with a new emblem, logo, or motto on them.

The Initial Command Inspection

All incoming company commanders are entitled to an Initial Command Inspection (ICI) within the first 90 days. The purpose is to provide you with written feedback on "the unit's strengths and weaknesses in relation to the higher headquarters' goals."[5] Coordinate with the S-3 to see if one has been scheduled. If not, contact the battalion commander. Don't miss out on an opportunity to establish a baseline that you can later compare your performance against.

Sometimes there simply isn't time in the training calendar to conduct an inspection within 90 days. If that is the case, write a memorandum for record stating what actions you took to pursue one and keep it on file. It may prove useful later.

Draft Required Policies

Army regulation requires commanders to develop several policies for their units.

- **Open Door Policy.** Soldiers have a duty to inform the commander of problems that affect discipline, morale, and mission effectiveness.[6] Your policy should inform soldiers how to do this.

---

[5] AR 1-201 §3-3c, 25 February 2015. The inspection areas are listed in Table B-2.
[6] AR 600-20 §2-2, 6 November 2014

- **Treatment of Persons**. Hazing and bullying are contrary to the Army's commitment to every person's dignity and respect. Commanders must emphasize a commitment to the proper treatment of persons and describe complaint procedures.[7]

- **Equal Opportunity (EO)**. This policy needs to emphasize your commitment and include protections from acts or threat of reprisal.[8]

- **Equal Opportunity Complaint Process**. A separate policy must list EO complaint procedures. AR 600-20, Appendix C details both formal and informal processes.

- **Prevention of Sexual Harassment (POSH).** This policy must explain both your commitment to prevention of sexual harassments and the complaint procedures[9]. Refer again to AR 600-20 Appendix C. EO and sexual harassment complaints follow similar procedures.

- **Prevention of Sexual Assault.** This policy letter must provide an overview of your commitment to the prevention of sexual assault as well as the Victim Advocacy Program. Include the definition of sexual assault, what resources are available to victims, and the fact that sexual assault is not only contrary to Army Values, but also a criminal offense under both the UCMJ and numerous federal and local civilian laws.[10]

---

[7] AR 600-20, §4-19c(2), 6 November 2014
[8] AR 600-20 §6-3i(11), 6 November 2014
[9] AR 600-20 §7-2b, 6 November 2014
[10] AR 600-20, §8-50(17), 6 November 2014

Command Climate Survey

Company commanders must administer a command climate survey within 30 days of taking command, after six months, and annually thereafter.[11] Contact the unit's Equal Opportunity Advisor prior to taking command in order to have the survey in place as soon as possible. In the survey, you will have the opportunity to select your own short answer questions. Choose the ones that address your particular areas of interest.

Schedule the Family Advocacy Briefing

If one of your soldiers has a serious incident at home, the military police will contact the Family Advocacy Program (FAP). Rather than wait until an emergency to learn about their mission, contact them to schedule their incoming commander's briefing. You are required to attend spouse and child abuse education program within 45 days of assuming command.[12]

Change of Command Inventory

These minor details lead up to the single most significant step prior to your assumption of command: the change of command inventory. This sizeable topic requires its own chapter.

---

[11] AR 600-20, §D-1a, 6 November 2014
[12] AR 600-20, §1-8b(1), 30 October 2007

CHANGE OF COMMAND
INVENTORY

"Unit assignments for officers, self-study, and professional military education comprise the three pillars of learning for our officers, but on the subject of property accountability little material exists for a self-study program..." —COL Thomas Rivard, The Army's Approach to Property Accountability: A Strategic Assessment, United States Army War College Class of 2012

This chapter is designed to fill in the self-study gap COL Rivard identified above. Strict adherence to the tenets of command supply discipline from the beginning will allow you to enforce high standards in your unit, distinguish yourself from your peers, reduce the risk of equipment loss, and avoid the mistakes that so many others have made.

To enforce high standards of supply discipline, you must understand the desired end state. It's not enough to simply look at all the equipment on the hand receipt and then sign the books. Before you sign the hand receipt, you must position yourself to attain the highest standards of supply accountability. Once you sit in the seat, the demands on your time will prevent significant improvements.

Before You Arrive

As mentioned previously, it's important to attend the Company Commanders/First Sergeants course before you take command. Once you've registered, your second step should be to contact the new unit's property book officer to ask for the Unit Identification Codes (UICs). This will allow you to research the unit before showing up.

1. Look up the UIC in FMS Web and get the MTOE/TDA. This will tell you what equipment the unit is supposed to have.

2. Get a Unit Asset Visibility Report (UAVR) from the unit. This will allow you to see how the equipment is allocated within the unit—significant deviances from the MTOE/TDA allocation can be either deliberate (due to mission), a sign the TDA needs to be updated, or an indicator of poor supply management.

3. Download a Tailored Index Report by UIC. This will tell you what TMs are applicable to what equipment.

4. Download all relevant Technical Manuals (TMs) using either the Tailored Index or ETMs Online for each National Stock Number (NSN). The TMs will show you what the Components of the End Item (COEI) and/or Basic Issue Items (BII) look like.

5. Check which items are Sets, Kits, and Outfits (SKOs), then download the component listings from ETMs Online.

6. Print sections from each TM that list COEI or BII. Put them in a binder to reference during the inventory.

If this sounds tedious, it is, but with the above documents you can do the following:

1. Compare the UAVR against the MTOE to identify excess, shortages, and allocations among sub-hand receipt holders.

2. Compare the Tailored Index Report against the UAVR to see which items have TMs.

3. Understand what items have COEI/BII and what those items look like.

This is important for several reasons. First, you never know what your unit's supply sergeant will be like, or how much experience they have. Second, by taking the time to research your company, you invest in your own ability to make good decisions as the company's primary Resource Manager. No matter how good your supply sergeant is, there are certain decisions that only you can make. Finally, what you learn will give you credibility with your supply sergeant. If nothing else, this process is a great opportunity to build your relationship.

On Arrival

You should expect three things when you meet with the outgoing commander: 1.) a schedule, 2.) a time to meet with your next higher commander to check for any instructions, and 3.) an orientation to the company's areas of operation. Even if you are familiar with the company's layout, there may still be areas you haven't seen before, so be sure to ask for a tour before you start the inventory. As you go over the schedule, check to see if it allows enough administrative time for the supply sergeant to draw up shortage annexes and component listings.

You should also expect a place to set up your workstation. You'll need:

- Computer, printer, and internet access

- Access to LIW

- File folder for each sub-hand receipt

- 4 differently colored highlighters

Preparing for the Inventory

Before beginning the inventory, sit down with the unit's Property Book Officer (PBO). There are a few "take-aways" you should get from the Change of Command Brief:

- The amount of time you have to complete the inventory. PBOs will typically tell you that you're allowed 30 days, with two extensions available on request.[1]

- You should identify excess items for turn-in and Found-On-Installation items that are physically on hand but unaccounted for.

- Get the list of required documents to complete the handover. This may include the list of items that don't have TMs, assumption of command orders, joint inventory statements, an after action report, etc. Be sure to get examples of what these look like.

- The PBO's phone number, in case something is not right, i.e. missing property, wrong serial numbers on sensitive items, or necessary personnel are not available (like the supply sergeant or the sub-hand receipt holders).

- The cyclic inventory schedule (by month, quarter, etc.)

- The Primary Hand Receipt, in two formats: Cyclic, and organized by Property Book Identification Code (PBIC)

- Copies of all sub-hand receipts.

- A divestiture report so you can identify what items may be obsolete.

With these items in hand, you should now mark your UAVR and sub-hand receipts to note the following:

---

[1] This is a widespread, but ultimately unit-specific practice. The timeline in DA Pam 710-2-1 §9-7c, 31 December 2007, applies only to PBO inventories.

1. Which items have subsystems, so you know when to refer to your Subsystems List.
2. How much BII each item has:
    a. No TM

    b. A TM, but no BII (some generators are like this)

    c. A little BII (like a generator with only a grounding rod)

    d. A lot of BII (like a P99881 CAISI antenna)

    e. A -10HR, for items like trucks that have preprinted 2062s in ETMs Online

    f. Sets, Kits, or Outfits (SKOs), like a T28688 General Mechanic Tool Kit.

3. Whether an item is required by MTOE or not.
4. Whether the unit is short or has an excess of any end items (and which hand receipt holder should be the one to turn theirs in).
5. Which month the equipment falls in for a cyclic inventory.
6. What items are obsolete, if any.

To blend the advantages of all these individual documents, carry around the following in a binder:

1. The marked-up copy of the UAVR.
2. The Subsystem List from the PBIC printout.
3. The marked up copies of the sub-hand receipts.
4. Several blank DA Form 2062s (or -10HRs, if possible), to document shortages.

As you look over the schedule and sub-hand receipts, you should get an idea how the inventory will be conducted. For each area, there are two approaches:

Method 1	Method 2
For common items or those with a lot of BII:	For low-density or serial numbered items:
1. By LIN	1. By Sub-Hand Receipt Holder
2. By Sub-Hand Receipt Holder	2. By LIN

Method 1. Take a medium truck company, for example. Since the platoons have essentially the same equipment, it makes sense for the whole company to lay out all M1083 Medium Tactical Vehicles (MTVs) with their associated BII at the same time. This way, you can properly identify all shortages and keep sub-hand receipt holders from sharing the same BII (ever seen the movie *Sergeant Bilko*?). This method works well with OE-254 antennas, M777 Howitzers, or anything else with numerous components distributed among multiple sub-hand receipt holders.

Method 2. Computers, armory equipment, and CBRN equipment are items can be effectively inventoried by individual sub-hand receipt holders. Since computers have serial numbers, sub-hand receipt holders can't trade them out. Other items, like weapon tripods, are held only by the armorer. Similarly, CBRN equipment is typically maintained by the unit CBRN specialist.

By understanding when to apply the two methods, you can identify "red flag" situations. If you find yourself looking at similar property from different hand receipt holders day after day, a red flag should go up in your head—why was this not all laid out at the same time? Is there an ongoing mission requirement, or was it simply poor planning? Are sub-hand receipt holders sharing BII? These kinds of observations should be reported to the PBO.

Organizational Clothing and Individual Equipment

The Army does not require commanders to perform an inventory of sol-diers' organizational clothing and individual equipment (OCIE) during the change of command inventory.[2] However, it may still be a unit-specific requirement.

Beginning the Inventory

From the first day, your actions and attitude will set the tone for the whole inventory. While the outgoing commander may have determined the schedule, in reality **you** will be the one who sets the pace. Here are some things to bear in mind:

- When possible, coordinate with the outgoing commander so the two of you can do the inventory together. See if they are interested in giving you input into how the process will occur and use this time to share your concerns and expectations.

- Before every day's activities, earmark the relevant TMs in your binder for quick reference.

- Conducting the inventory with the outgoing commander can become stressful. You may be working with a commander who has not maintained accountability and/or is disorganized. I recom-mend conducting the first inventory according to the outgoing commander's plan. If you see that it is not organized, individuals are not well prepared, or that they are not sure of the compo-nents themselves, then suggest a discussion with the outgoing commander to review expectations.

- Don't think problems won't come up. Inventories that should have taken no more than two hours have taken eight. In a profes-

---

[2] DA Pam 710-2-1 §10-8 and §10-10, 31 December 2007, state that OCIE inventories must be done on arrival at a unit and before clearing the installation.

sional and calm demeanor, express to the outgoing commander that you would appreciate the next day's inventory to follow the procedures outlined above. If necessary, delay the next inspections to allow the elements to prepare for the inspection. The last thing you want to do is waste your time and your Soldiers' time. If the first set of inventories did not go well it is likely the outgoing commander might be embarrassed or defensive. Be prepared for this when you engage in conversation. Set the conversation in a manner that shows you are trying to reduce their liability and complete the inventory quickly and professionally. This allows you to report to the battalion commander how smooth the process was, allowing the outgoing commander to seem like a hero. Some battalion commanders will hold the outgoing commander's evaluation until the change of command is complete.

- As the incoming commander, this process will also give you an indication on which elements of your unit are organized and which are lacking. Make notes so you can follow up with any necessary training.

- Be professional, fair, and courteous. This is the first interaction your Soldiers will have with you. Make it a positive one. Failure to do so could result in Soldiers not wanting to share information with you or feeling that you don't care. Either way, it would be a bad start and a difficult perception to overcome.

- Ensure each hand receipt holder has the current TM (this is especially important for vehicles). The right TM will list each part's NSN and provide a picture and description of the items you are inventorying. Do not make the mistake of allowing someone to convince you that what you are looking at is the correct item. There is a big difference between a 5 inch flathead screwdriver and a 5 inch *nonmetallic* flat head screwdriver. Sometimes the difference can be hundreds or thousands of dollars. So be careful—once you sign for it, you own it.

- At the end of each day, do a "hot-wash" to review what you've seen and what you didn't have time for. Make notes for your AAR on how long it took to go through what you did. This information will be important when you schedule the cyclic inventories and again as you finish command.

- When you come across excess equipment, ask these questions before you decide to turn it in:

  o Who remembers how the unit received this property?

  o Do you have any historical documentation?

  o If you cannot verify the purpose of this piece of property considering contacting the previous commander, ask the supply sergeant or S4 to contact their predecessor.

  o (To the hand receipt holder) Does this piece of property help you with any part of your current or standby mission?

  o What would the unintended consequences be if we turned this in?

  o Who should we tell if we turn this in?

  o Should you seek guidance from the S4, BN XO, or BN CDR? (This is key for HHCs.)

- If the unit has significant amounts of excess or useless equipment, it might be an indication the unit was ordered to take on this property (perhaps due to another unit's closure) and no turn in plan was developed. If this is the case, develop, coordinate, and execute a turn in plan with the supply sergeant.

- Before turning in excess equipment, ensure that the equipment is not needed to execute the unit's mission. Sometimes equipment is picked up for a specialized mission modification and not turned in or not reflected on the TDA. The last thing you want to do is turn in property only to find out you actually needed it.

Handling a Sub-par Supply Sergeant

A good supply sergeant can almost literally be worth their weight in gold. Yet professionalism in the 92Y MOS is not uniform across the Army. Good management requires knowing how to handle less-than-ideal circumstances.

- *An Inexperienced Supply Sergeant:* Some units have received recently re-classed E-4 Specialists to fill an E-5 Sergeant slot—hardly a perfect substitution. If you have an inexperienced supply sergeant, make a list of the critical skills you want them to be proficient in. Coordinate with the S4's Senior Supply Sergeant or another unit commander/supply team to have these skills trained to standard. Properly executed, the supply sergeant will see this as you taking an interest in their professional.

- *A Poor or Incompetent Supply Sergeant:* If you have any issues with the credibility, trust, or competency of your supply sergeant, it is wise to address them immediately with formal counseling. Develop a plan of action to fix the issues you have observed. Counsel the individual monthly. This shows the individual that you are tracking the issues and trying to help them grow. If it comes down to a relief action or a less than stellar evaluation report there will be no questions asked because you have documented the issues and followed through with your plan of action. Make sure that you complete the Assessment (Part IV of the DA Form 4856) from previous monthly performance counseling statements before giving the next counseling statement. Consider seeking guidance from the 1SG, S4, BN CSM, and/or other Company Commanders. If you're noticing a problem at this stage, you're probably not the first.

Shortage Annexes and Component Listings

In order to meet the requirement that all authorized equipment be on hand or on request, you'll have to record which items are missing (so that you can order them) while also ensuring that items currently on hand don't somehow go missing. This will require you and your supply team to generate shortage annexes and component hand receipts.[3]

In this day and age of computerized inventory processes, procedures from the 1997 version of DA PAM 710-2-1 may seem out-dated. Because automated systems had yet to take hold in every unit, those procedures had you make duplicates, keep originals, and maintain records in filing cabinets. These days, adhering to such practices seems almost archaic.

"When an end item issued on a change document has component shortages, prepare a hand receipt annex (para 6–1) to document the missing components."—DA PAM 710-2-1 §5-3d(1), 31 December 1997.

Nevertheless, there's something to be said for the old ways. While true that many inventory processes can be done electronically, redundancy is the hallmark of diligence (when it comes to supply, at least). Maintaining all original paper copies and change documents on file remains a best practice. This will allow you to establish control, keep visibility of all supply transactions involving sub-hand receipt holders, and independently confirm your supply sergeant's automated transactions.

---

[3] DA Pam 710-2-1 §6-1 and §6-2, 31 December 2007

To make sure you and your supply sergeant are on the same page, create digital backups, scan all documents (saving them locally in organized folders) and email copies to both the supply sergeant and the sub-hand receipt holder involved. This will provide a back-up "virtual paper trail" in case you lose one format of your records.

This is particularly important when managing shortage annexes (also called hand receipt annexes) and component hand receipts. The shortage annexes you create during your change of command inventory will be useful for ordering and tracking replacement parts throughout your command time. The mirror image of the shortage annex, the component listing, is how you track what items a sub-hand receipt holder actually has on hand. Expressed in math terms, it would look like this: (TM listed components) - (Items on the Shortage Annex) = (Component Listing).

You may ask, "Why bother with a component listing if I've already got the shortage annex? Isn't that double work?" The answer is *because your sub-hand receipt holders should further sub-hand receipt equipment down to the user level.* The shortage annexes are needed for ordering shortages; component listings are needed for issuing equipment down to the user level.

By drawing up DA Form 2062 component listings in PDF format, you simplify the process for your sub-hand receipt holders. Rather than retyping every line, they can reprint the same component listings. DA PAM 710-2-1 Figure 6-2 shows how this looks.

Ideally, the outgoing commander or supply sergeant would already have these drawn up and on hand as you are doing the inventory. If that's the case, then you need only confirm that each sub-hand receipt holder's shortage annexes are accurate and ensure they have signed the component listing.

If these documents are not available, then you will have to start from the beginning. And *yes,* this will be a pain in the neck, but it *must* get done—and doing it at the beginning will make your cyclic inventories infinitely easier. In this situation, use blank 2062s to note each missing item, then—at the end of each day—consolidate them to create one shortage annex per sub-hand receipt holder per NSN. Sign each one and give copies to the supply sergeant to (later) place on order.

Once you've generated the shortage annexes, compile them in file folders by hand receipt holder. Mark off on your master Primary Hand Receipt what you saw, using different color highlighters to note each item's status:

- **Green:** end item on hand with no shortages.
- **Yellow:** end item on hand with shortages.
- **Orange:** end item on hand but unserviceable.
- **Pink:** Item on hand but is excess or obsolete and should be turned in.

Finally, check in with the outgoing commander every few days to communicate whether you are on schedule or if you need to submit an extension request.

Ensuring Accountability

Consider the following best practice.

- Hand receipt holders and sub hand receipt holders to bring their individual hand receipts to each day's events. At the end of your inventory your HR should match the hand receipt holder's and sub hand receipt holder's information exactly. If not, re-verify the information until everyone has the same numbers.

- When all components are laid out (for example, vehicles with their BII), have the hand receipt holders and the sub hand receipt holders can sign their new hand receipts (from you) right then and there. Another option is to wait until all paperwork is updated and then have the individuals sign their hand receipts.

- If you catch individuals sharing equipment, address this when you officially take command. At a minimum make a note of the incident and the individuals involved.

- Color code each section's equipment to prevent cross contamination or sharing of property. Assign each platoon its own color code, and each squad a particular shape (a band, square, triangle, etc.). Have each squad mark their equipment with their shape and color to quickly identify what belongs to whom.

Wrapping Up

Any items (whether end items, components, or BII) left unseen and unrecorded on a shortage annex at the end of the schedule require a relief document—either a cash collection voucher, a statement of charges, or the dreaded DD Form 200 Financial Liability Investigation of Property Loss (FLIPL). The outgoing commander or supply sergeant will handle this; your part is to maintain your own records. This way, you have recourse if anything *else* goes missing by the time the cyclic inventory comes around.

After everything is accounted for by one means or another, the outgoing commander typically develops the out brief for review by higher echelons. While you won't have too much of a speaking role in these meetings, you should take note what is discussed—you will have your turn in due time.

Before other events overtake you, make some notes for future evaluations—both others' and yours. If a platoon leader identified $100,000 worth of excess property during change of command inventory, have that platoon leader turn it in—it's an excellent bullet point on an OER. And don't be afraid to do the include the same information on yours. "Reduced excess property by $150,000 within 60 days of assuming command" sends a strong message that you know what you're doing.

Be sure to type up your notes on how things went, how long the total process took, and what mistakes to avoid when you finish command. Include observations, issues, commendations, pats on the back, and areas for focused training. This will not only help you when looking for professional development ideas, but also help facilitate the process for the next commander.

Going Forward

Once the change of command is approved, you'll sit down with the PBO and formally sign the property books, assuming responsibility for all property. Looking ahead, your ability to enforce good property management will hinge on your ability to complete four responsibilities:

1. **Cyclic inventories**. Schedule these on your training calendar and perform them monthly.
2. **Sub Hand Receipt Holder training**. So that they know how to manage their own property.
3. **Property allocation**. To ensure the right people have the right equipment.
4. **Ordering shortages and maintaining shortage annexes.** To decrease your overall shortage levels.

The Resource Manager chapter describes these topics further, but at this point there's nothing holding you back from the change of command ceremony.

Arranging the Reception

The timeline for a company-level change of command depends on both the inventory process and the brigade commander's schedule. You may affect the former, but you can't fully control either. Regardless when the ceremony takes place, you'll be expected to host a reception and provide food.

The reception location may be the company common area or an on-post event hall. Keep the food simple and in-line with the expected number of attendees. Government funds may be available for the cake, but check on this first. Large cakes are usually available at the commissary. The orderly room should draw up the programs and send out invitations to official guests.

Conclusion

By this point, you'll have done everything you can to start things off right. Now let's look at how to maintain your good start.

Example Cyclic Schedule

DEPARTMENT OF THE ARMY
HEADQUARTERS, 501ˢᵗ SUSTAINMENT BRIGADE
UNIT # 15476
APO AP 96260-5476

[OFFICE SYMBOL]   14 April 2015

MEMORANDUM FOR ALL PRIMARY HAND RECEIPT HOLDERS

SUBJECT: Monthly Cyclic (10%) Inventory Schedule

1. Army Regulation require that all Primary Hand Receipt Holders will conduct a 100% physical inventory of all equipment in their unit each year. In accordance with AR 710-2 table 2-2 (b), DA Pam 710-2-1 Chap 9-6, the cyclic inventory method has been chosen for use in this command.

2. During the period of January (when no cyclic inventory is due) units will inventory all durable items to include office furniture and ensure it is hand receipted to the user per DA Pam 710-2-1 Chap 4-1, 5-1(C2), 5-3(A&B); CTA 50-909 Chap 14. A memorandum acknowledging completion of this action is required to the PBO office NLT 31 January.

3. The assigned inventory schedule for the 501ˢᵗ SBDE is:

Month	Due NLT	Cyclic Range / Durable Review
January	25-Jan	Annual Durable Review Memorandum (SKO / Tool Kits)
February	25-Feb	I00000 thru JZ9999
March	25-Mar	K00000 thru MZ9999
April	25-Apr	N00000 thru PZ9999
May	25-May	Q00000 thru RZ9999
June	25-Jun	S00000 thru ZZ9999
July	25-Jul	000000 thru 9ZZZZZ
August	25-Aug	N/A (UFG)
September	25-Sep	A00000 thru DZ9999
October	25-Oct	E00000 thru FZ9999
November	25-Nov	G00000 thru HZ9999
December	25-Dec	N/A (Start January Review of Durable Items)

4. The point of contact for this memorandum is the undersigned at [PHONE NUMBER].

[SIGNATURE BLOCK]

Shortage Annex Example

HAND RECEIPT/ANNEX NUMBER For use of this form, see DA PAM 710-2-1; The proponent agency is ODCSLOG.		FROM: Commander, HHC, 498th CSSB	TO: SASMO NCOIC, SSG Parra, Felix				HAND RECEIPT NUMBER ORG SASMO	
FOR ANNEX OR ONLY	END ITEM STOCK NUMBER F55621, 6150-01-308-5671	END ITEM DESCRIPTION Power Distribution, M100 A/P	PUBLICATION NUMBER TM 9-6150-226-13		PUBLICATION DATE 15 APRIL 2012		QUANTITY 1	
STOCK NUMBER a.	ITEM DESCRIPTION b.		* c.	SEC d.	UI e.	QTY AUTH f.	QUANTITY g.	
							A	B	C	D	E	F
6150-01-598-5282	CENTER, ELECTRICAL FEEDER: 3-phase 120/208 V, 100-amp/ph (97403) P/N 13329J E6325					1	1					
6150-01-256-6300	CABLE, PIGTAIL: 100-amp, 4-ft (1.2m), 8-pin (97403) P/N 13226E7020					1	1					
6150-01-256-6304	CABLE, SERVICE/FEEDER: 100-amp, 50-ft (15.2 m), 8-pin (97403) P/N 13226E7024					2	2					
6150-01-256-6299	STRAP DOUBLE, CABLE CARRYING (97403) P/N 13227E5821					4	4					

* WHEN USED AS A:

HAND RECEIPT, enter Hand Receipt Annex Number
HAND RECEIPT FOR QUARTERS FURNITURE, enter Condition Codes
HAND RECEIPT ANNEX/COMPONENTS RECEIPT, enter Accounting Requirements Code (ARC).

DA FORM 2062, JAN 1982   EDITION OF JAN 58 IS OBSOLETE   PAGE _____ OF _____ PAGES   APD LC v2.10

List of Property Pending Disposition Example

Book	LIN	Desc	Qty	Reason
TDA	70320N	COMPUTER PALMTOP AC/DC ADAPTER: CK31 INT	8	excess
TDA	B67839	M24 BINOCULAR	6	excess
TDA	E68694	CMP UT REP AIR	1	obsolete, excess
TDA	FG301A	SPECTROMETER, CHROMATO-GRAPH/MASS: FIRSTD	1	excess
TDA	FG6526	IDENTIFINDER-NG: UNDERWA-TER VERSION GOVE	1	excess
TDA	FG6558	HAZMAT ID: 023-1010 SMITHS DETECTIONS	1	excess
TDA	R97234	RIFLE 5.56 MM M4	10	excess
TDA	S45729	SIGHT BORE OPT M150	3	excess
TDA	S60288	SIGHT REFLEX COLLIMA	22	excess
TDA	S65581	SIG GEN	2	obsolete, unservice-able
TDA	V64052	TEST SET ARMU A/V IND	1	obsolete, excess
TDA	V78026	TEST ST GEN-VOLT REG	1	obsolete, excess
TDA	W51910	TOOL KIT,REPAIRMAN'S,SMALL ARMS	1	obsolete
TDA	W89557	TRCTR WHL WHSE DED PT	1	obsolete
ORG	63039N	POLISHER,FLOOR,ELECTRIC	1	excess
ORG	70223N	CONTROL-MONITOR	1	wrong LIN? excess
ORG	98406N	STRAPPING AND SEALING KIT	2	excess
ORG	B60351	BORESIGHT EQUIP M30	1	obsolete, excess
ORG	C05701	IMPROVED CHEM AGT MON	3	obsolete, excess

The following documents for this chapter are available online:

- Example Joint After Action Review Memo

- Example New Commander List of Hand Receipt Holders

- Example Joint Inventory Statement

- Example List of Items without TMs (ORG + TDA + Installation)

- Example New Commander Statement Accepting Property Responsibility (Template)

- Example SubHand Receipt Holder Responsibility Statement Template

- Example Assumption of Command memo (AR 600-20 Figure 2-2)

- Example Assumption of Command memo (Word format)

- Example Cyclic inventory schedule

- Example How to mark up your Unit Asset Visibility Report

- Example Justification not to Order Shortages

- Example List of Turn-ins and Transfers

- Example Master Divestiture Listing for Korea for 19th ESC (Marked Up)

- Example Memorandum For Record (MFR)

- Example of what Documents You Should Put into a Binder

- Example PBUSE—Generated Reconciliation

- Example Property Book—Cyclic Format (MTOE)

- Example Property Book—PBIC Format (MTOE)

- Example Property Book by Sub-Hand Receipt Holders MTOE

- Example Property Book by Sub-Hand Receipt Holders TDA

- Example Shortage Annex F55621 Signed

- Example Shortage Annex F55621 Unsigned

- Example TM - F55621 just COEI and BII pages

- Example Unit Asset Visibility Report MTOE (Not Marked Up)

- Example Unit Asset Visibility Report TDA (Not Marked Up)

- Sample MTOE Equipment (One Page)

- Sample MTOE Personnel (One Page)

- Sample Tailored Report by UIC - WCBK99 (TDA)

- Sample Tailored Report by UIC - WCBKAA (MTOE)

View available documents at: asktop.net/mocc

Password: 88YEZX9

PART II: MANAGING A COMPANY

OK, I thought to myself, I did it. I'm a company commander. So, what does a company commander do?

Knowing your job does not make you a great leader, but great leaders are invariably "technically and tactically proficient." Managers are measured a little differently—the great ones not only know their own jobs, but can train subordinates in their jobs as well.

As a company commander, everything you do will fit into one of five major roles:

1. Administrator
2. Resource Manager
3. Conscience/Counselor/Coach
4. Hammer
5. Training Manager

In the following sections, we'll look at what each of these roles means, what your part is, and what you can reasonably expect from your subordinates.

5

ADMINISTRATOR

> *"Captains must arrive prepared, or they will not be able to make the most of their experience. Many officers think they are prepared, but are quickly overwhelmed by the administrative responsibilities that come along with being a company commander."—Joe Byerly, From the Green Notebook*[1]

The company commander is the chief administrator for the company. In this role, the commander ensures all personnel-related actions are processed in a timely basis. There are two types of actions: regularly recurring action, and *ad hoc* actions performed on as-needed basis.

Regularly Recurring Actions

At various time throughout the month, you must submit the following:

- PERSTATs (Daily to S1)

- Unit Commanders Finance report (Early in the month, S1)

- Monthly Reports (Early in the month, S1)

---

[1] https://fromthegreennotebook.com/2015/10/10/how-to-get-the-most-out-of-company-command/

- Human Resources Authorization Report (Semi-monthly, S1)

- Unit Status Reports (Early in the month, Battalion additional duty officer)

- Updates of DD93, SGLV, and records reviews (Ongoing, S1)

- Duty Rosters (Monthly, Internal)

- Rating Scheme (Ongoing, Internal)

How to do the PERSTATs (Due daily to S1)

The Personnel Status (PERSTAT) report is straightforward, and requires little input from the commander. Every day, the Personnel Actions Clerk (PAC) must submit the duty status of every soldier to the S1. [2] Ensure the PAC keeps a record.

How to do the Unit Financial Transaction Report (UCFR) (Due early in the month to S1)

Every month, the finance office generates a list of assigned soldiers showing their base pay, housing rates, accrued leave, and allotments total. The commander's job is to review the UCFR on a monthly basis and report discrepancies.[3] Since late 2015, the report has been handled digitally.

Once the PAC receives the UCFR, they add the "assigned-but-not-listed" personnel and notate the " listed-but-not-assigned personnel." After the PAC forwards it for review, the executive officer and first sergeant should go over the report, looking for soldiers who either have high leave balances, are receiving BAS or incentive pay incorrectly, have incurred new debts (through casual pays), are AWOL or under Article 15 punishments, or have changes in their marital status.

---

[2] AR 600-8-6 §1-24b, 1 April 2015
[3] AR 37-104-4 §1-4g

Once discrepancies have been identified and the proper paperwork is ready for the S1, digitally sign the UCFR online. Maintain digital copies of the report as well as the supporting documentation. Follow up with the S1 to ensure everything is in order, and note the corrections that had to be made. It may take a few cycles for changes to take effect.

> Watch soldiers' marital status closely. Without an exception to policy, sergeants (E-5) may be required to live in barracks if they have no dependents or they have custody of children for less than half of the year. Identify recently divorced parents in your formation early so that you can both prevent financial difficulties and avoid "no pay due" situations.

How to do the Monthly Reports (Due early in the month to S1)

Early each month, you must sign off on several personnel reports:

- AAA-162, Unit Personnel Accountability Report. Each soldier's duty status should be accurate.

- AAA-167, Unit Soldier Readiness Report. Check the DD93 and SGLV dates, as well as the medical status.

- AAA-199, Good Conduct Medal Roster. This report lists who is eligible for another good conduct medal. Be sure not to approve any flagged personnel, and be sure to recognize qualified recipients in a formation (especially first-time recipients).

- AAA-160, Report of AWOLs. This report lists the soldiers whose duty status is Absent, Without Leave.

- AAA-165, Unit Personnel Accountability Notices. In overseas locations, this report will show personnel who have been kept past their DEROS.

- AAA-095, Suspension of Favorable Actions Management Report. Also known as the flag report, this shows who is currently flagged as well as soldiers who have graduated from the Army Body Composition Program within the past 36 months.

- AAA-117, Enlisted Advancement Report (for junior enlisted personnel). With this report, you choose which eligible soldiers (E-1 to E-3) may be promoted. Those in the primary zone may be promoted without a waiver, while those in the secondary zone may only be promoted if you have a waiver available. Note that if you deny a primary zone promotion, the soldier's first-line leader must counsel them, in writing, on what deficiencies need to be corrected.[4]

- AAA-294, Enlisted Promotion Report (For promotion to E-5 and E-6). Promotion to sergeant and staff sergeant is semi-centralized, meaning promotion is determined by several factors. You can defer to the first sergeant's guidance on who is qualified.

To ensure equity and transparency in promotions, ask the first sergeant to develop a standing operating procedure that explains how waivers are granted. To ensure decisions are fair and consistent, require that all promotions be agreed upon by the first sergeant and platoon sergeants together. This way, if the consensus is that a primary zone soldier should not be promoted, the platoon sergeant and first line supervisor will be able to knowledgeably write up the counseling.

How to do the Unit Status Reports (Early in the month, Battalion additional duty officer)

NetUSR is one of the Defense Readiness Reporting System—Army (DRRS-A) suite of applications by which units report their readiness status.

---

[4] AR 600-8-19 §1-27, 18 December 2015

Higher echelons compile this data to gauge how prepared a units are for potential deployments.

Because the data entry process requires a significant amount of time, executive officers typically complete report on the commander's behalf. However, a commander must be able to brief the unit's current status and explain any changes from the previous month.

One company commander told the executive officer not to slot personnel in NetUSR—that the first sergeant was the only person authorized to do this. Given the disconnect between eMilpo and DRRS-A, this was complete nonsense. The XO knew it, and politely ignored the commander. If you haven't used NetUSR before, run through the process for a couple months. You must understand how processes work to give meaningful input.

Based on information drawn from various Army systems, NetUSR measures the unit's personnel (P), equipment (S), maintenance (R), and training (T) statuses, each ranked by a number representing a certain "tier." For instance, an "S1" means you have virtually all your MTOE equipment. A "P4," on the other hand, means you are woefully short of MTOE required personnel. The staff proponent that collects and consolidates the data may vary, but it often falls to the S2 for no other reason that it involves classified information.[5]

Some ratings are fairly objective. The personnel, equipment, and maintenance ratings are determined according to specific formulae. However, the Mission Essential Task List assessment and training status are much more subjective.

Also, the quality of the reporting process varies by unit. Some battalions seek a very high degree of accuracy, and require the S1 and S4 staff sec-

---

[5] AR 220-1 §11-1d, 15 April 2010. Secret at the battalion level; confidential at the company level.

tions to scrutinize supporting paperwork. In this case, the S1 will review soldiers' profiles (looking to see which ones expire by the 15th of the month), check who is promotable, and review the gains roster to verify personnel shortages. In these units, the process can take an entire day.

Other units are less meticulous. With the AAA-162, AAA-167, and previous month's Army Materiel Status System (AMSS) report, an experienced person can finish in less than two hours. The difference reflects the emphasis placed on the process from higher up.

Regardless, the technical aspects of data entry are less important than the human interactions underlying the process. NetUSR's "Validate" function will specify what errors need correction, but it can't help in determining what personnel and equipment shortages merit the battalion commander's attention. Before any briefing with the battalion commander, synchronize with the S-1 and S-4 so that you can present a unified recommendation.

Some other notes about DRRS-A:

1. Report honestly. "No commander is expected to achieve or report a unit readiness status that is higher than that possible with the resources made available to him. All commanders at all times will submit timely, accurate, and complete reports that neither exaggerate nor mask unit readiness deficiencies."[6] The unit status report is not a performance report card.

2. You must report the training and capability status of for each of the Mission Essential Tasks (METs) on the unit's standard Full Spectrum Operations MET List.[7] (This can be found on the Army Training Network.[8]) However, you must also discuss with the battalion commander what the unit's training focus should be, since some training objectives will naturally outweigh others.

---

[6] AR 220-1, §7-1b, 15 April 2010
[7] AR 220-1 §B-3b, 15 April 2010. Current doctrine now calls this Unified Land Operations
[8] https://atn.army.mil/ Follow the links Unit Training Management > Enablers > Mission Essential Task List.

3. HHCs with AA-level UICs must report the battalion commander's assessment of the headquarters rather the company commander's assessment of the company. To do this, the HHC commander must coordinate with the battalion commander *before* beginning the report.[9]

4. Obsolete equipment (as determined by a master divestiture list from the property book office) may not be counted toward an authorization, even if it remains on the property book.[10]

5. Turnover during the summer months will be higher than normal, so it's important to report this percentage correctly. Turnover should be reported as the number of departures *over the past three months* divided by the current number of assigned personnel.[11]

DRRS-A presents leaders with an interesting ethical dilemma, particularly as the Army shifts focus from the ARFORGEN deployment cycle to contingency operations. Commanders are tasked to "build ready units"[12] while also reporting how ready they are. No area illustrates this conflict of interest better than how a unit deals with obsolete equipment. Obsolete equipment must not be included in S-level calculations, even if it remains on the property book.[13] Yet higher level commanders may be tempted to keep the S-level higher by including them, and neither NetUSR nor any staff sections will detect an error. The unit will not register a shortage because the property remains on the books, and higher echelons will be unaware there is any problem until the unit is called upon to conduct a contingency operation.

---

[9] AR 220-1 §8-4c, 15 April 2010
[10] AR 220-1 §9-3d(1), 15 April 2010
[11] AR 220-1 §9-2h(1), 15 April 2010

How to do the Human Resources Authorization Report (AAA-161) (Semimonthly)

Formerly called the Unit Manning Report, this eMILPO-generated report compares unit strength levels against the unit's Modified Table of Organization and Equipment (MTOE). Let the first sergeant handle the slotting, but you should be familiar with some of the rules.

- Assigned soldiers may not be double-slotted.[14]

- Incoming assigned soldiers must be assigned within 7 days after arrival to an MTOE slot, or be recognized as "Reassignable Overstrength"[15]

- AWOL soldiers should be dropped from the roles on the 31st day of AWOL[16] This requires that the PERSTATs accurately show the soldier's duty status is "AWL" as soon as possible[17]

- Soldiers in civil confinement for at least 6 must be removed.

Practices vary, but the S-1 is required to produce the report semi-monthly for unit commander's verification.

Updating DD93, SGLV, and records reviews (Ongoing, S1)

Commanders "must take deliberate steps to ensure the accuracy of soldier records as they have a significant impact on Army promotion and/or selection boards, assignment opportunities, and financial audit readiness for the Army."[18] This requires verification via the S1's Record Review Tool. In addition, soldiers must update their DD Form 93 (Record of Emergency Data) and SGLV 8286 (Servicemembers' Group Life Insurance Election and Certificate) at least annually.

---

[12] http://www.usarak.army.mil/main/Stories_Archives/Jan_22-25_2013/130122_FS1.asp
[13] AR 220-1 §9-3d, 15 April 2010
[14] AR 600-8-6 § 3-18e, 1 April 2015
[15] AR 600-8-6 §3-18d, 1 April 2015
[16] AR 600-8-6 §3-12a, 1 April 2015
[17] AR 600-8-6 Table 2-1, 1 April 2015
[18] AR 600-8-104 §3-7, 7 April 2014

The best way to track these actions is with an Excel spreadsheet showing when everyone last completed each task. The S1 can easily generate this for the entire battalion. If there's no other SOP, have platoons to send their soldiers the S1 shop at around the 11-month mark, and provide visibility on this with the spreadsheet. You can do this fairly easily with an Excel formula.[19]

How to review duty rosters

Drawing up the duty rosters is the first sergeant's lane, but as the company commander, you remain accountable for making sure duties are assigned equitably throughout the unit. Use of DA Form 6 is mandatory.[20]

If duties are assigned month-by-month, decide the date by which you want them published. The first sergeant should submit the rosters for approval in memo format, along with the DA Form 6s, a few days beforehand. Review, sign, and post the rosters on a bulletin board. Maintain files of both the DA Form 6s and the final memos.

How to do the Rating Scheme

The commander is responsible for publishing a rating scheme that includes every rated soldier.[21] The rating scheme should be posted in a public place and updated every time a rated NCO or officer either arrives or departs the unit.

While the S1 usually handles the rating schemes for commissioned and warrant officers, rating schemes for NCOs are handled at the company level. These are the directions for determining the rating scheme for your company's NCOs:

---

[19] Excel can handle formulae with dates. In this case, the formula would be "=A1+330" where A1 is the last date of completion.
[20] AR 220-45 §4c
[21] AR 623-3 §1-4b(5), 4 November 2015

1. Print the AAA-167, which includes all assigned and attached NCOs (E5+) and shows their MOSs.

2. Determine their MTOE positions (if unsure, ask the first sergeant). If a sergeant is not in an MTOE slot, list their job function (e.g. Training Room NCO).

3. Determine each one's Rater, Senior Rater, and Reviewer.

   a. Senior raters must be the rater's rater.[22]

   b. Senior raters must meet specified rank requirements. [23]

   c. Personnel detached from your unit should be contacted for rating chain information.

4. Look up each rated NCO's last evaluation date on the Evaluation Reporting Website[24] and determine each one's next evaluation date.[25] There are essentially three reasons for an evaluation:

   a. Annual and Extended Annual. These require the NCO to be in the same position with the same rater for one full year.

   b. Change of rater. A change of rater evaluation is due by the THRU date if the rater had 90 days or more of rated time, but less than a full year. (Overseas areas with fixed DEROS dates make it easy to track these dates.) Compare the NCO's departure/THRU dates against their rater's. The rater should submit the NCOER for review no later than 45 days prior to whomever's is first.

   c. Ad hoc and optional evaluations[26]. Examples include Change of Duty, Complete the Record, and Relief for Cause. These will not be shown in the rating scheme, and are much less common than the other two types.

---

[22] AR 623-3 §2-7(b)(3), 4 November 2015
[23] AR 623-3 Table 2-1, 4 November 2015
[24] https://cops.hrc.army.mil/
[25] https://knoxhrc16.hrc.army.mil/iwrs/
[26] The full list of evaluation types is listed in AR 623-3 Section VIII.

5. Use an Excel spreadsheet to enter the data. This will allow you to sort by rank, last name, or by due date as required.

Senior raters should also be forewarned when a Senior Rater Option evaluation is due. For example, if a soldier's senior rater leaves on June 30th and their rater leaves one month later on July 31st, the rater may have met the requirement for 90 days of rated time, but the new senior rater will not. In this case, the old senior rater completes the senior rater portion.[27]

Certain positions have special considerations. Battalion career counselors must be rated by the command sergeant major.[28] An NCO serving as a battalion's full-time SHARP representative will have to be rated directly by the battalion commander if the brigade commander wants to be in the rating chain. And if the battalion commander's driver is an NCO, they will have to be rated by either a major, the HHC commander, or the command sergeant major for the battalion commander to be the senior rater.

Ad hoc Actions

The following actions are done on an as-needed basis following some sort of change:

- Reports of Unfavorable Information for Security Determination (DA Form 5248s, due to S2)

- Personnel Asset Inventories (After company and battalion changes of command)

- Leave/Pass Requests

- DA Form 4187 Personnel Actions

---

[27] AR 623-3 §3-57c, 4 November 2015
[28] AR 601-280 §9-6e, 31 January 2006

Reports of Unfavorable Information for Security Determination (DA Form 5248s, due to S2)

For security purposes, the S-2 has an interest in all founded and even alleged misconduct that might affect a security clearance. If you learn of credible derogatory information about a soldier[29], whether they currently have a clearance or not, you must submit an initial DA Form 5248-R to the battalion security manager.[30] As the matter is closed, positively or negatively, submit a closure report detailing the actions taken.

Most 5248-Rs will be for "Disregard of Regulations" following an Article 15[31], but there are other situations when one is required. Acts of poor judgment, excessive indebtedness, and dishonesty are among the specifically listed examples.[32]

Once submitted, save all DA Form 5248-Rs in a digital folder.

Personnel Asset Inventories (after company and battalion changes of command, to S1)

Every unit that is assigned a unique Unit Identification Code must conduct a PAI after a change in command. [33] Just as commanders must account for all assigned property, so also must they account for all assigned and attached personnel.

Allow the first sergeant to set the time and place for the physical muster of assigned and attached personnel. The PAI must consist of the following actions:

- Reconcile the physical muster against the AAA-162 personnel roster. Account for personnel not present. (This is usually assigned to the PAC).

---

[29] AR 380-67 §2-4 and Appendix I, 24 January 2014, list the criteria
[30] AR 380-67 §8-2, 24 January 2014
[31] AR 380-67 §2-4g, 24 January 2014
[32] AR 380-67 Appendix I offers the best details on what is of interest.
[33] AR 600-8-6 §5-7a(1), 1 April 2015

- Ensure DA Form 3986 is used to document the results (the PAC can submit this through the first sergeant).

- Sign the 3986 and send to the S1. Keep a digital copy in your records.

Leave/Pass requests

Commanders must establish an annual leave program that provides soldiers maximum opportunity for them to take leave. The goal is to minimize leave day lost and payouts of leave not taken, while also contributing positively to morale, level of performance, and career motivation.[34]

In addition, a strong pass program provides incentives for positive performance. Soldiers should be encouraged to perform well on PT tests, reenlist, and compete in boards (e.g. soldiers of the quarter/year).

If the battalion commander has not already established a pass policy, create one yourself. Include vehicle safety inspections and a travel radius within which soldiers don't need a pass. Your soldiers will appreciate it, and your boss will, too.

The process by which a soldier requests leave or pass should be simple and transparent, so develop a standing operating procedure (SOP) that lists requirements. If you want all soldiers to complete a host of requirements before you'll approve, it's best to let them know far in advance. And to reduce differences in policies, communicate with other company commanders—no commander likes having to answer why things are better over in Company X.

Finally, note that while passes are granted for positive performance of duty, leave is earned. While you have the authority to deny leave requests, taking leave is not a "favorable action" that a flag would preclude.

[34] AR 600-8-10 §2-1, 15 February 2006

DA Form 4187 Personnel Actions

There are 8 gazillion soldier actions that require a commander's signature, from taking a language test to getting permission to retire. All of them should be successfully handled in a timely manner or returned to the submitter for corrections.

How fast is "timely"? For some commanders it's 24 hours. For others it can be 72, depending on the operations tempo. Whatever you decide, stress to your first sergeant, executive officer, and PAC that the accurate and expedient processing of soldier paperwork is among the best ways to build morale in the unit. Soldiers have no choice but to trust you with their issues—don't violate that trust.

To help close the circle, tell your soldiers that if they haven't heard back on their action within a week they need to follow up on it—no one should be holding on to paperwork. For your part, your orderly room must follow up with the S1 to ensure they are also doing their part. Your headquarters' responsibilities to the soldier don't end at hitting the Send button.

At the same time, the orderly room's highest priorities do not always need to be *your* number one priority. Stephen Covey's timeless book *First Things First* offers the "Big Rock" anecdote to illustrate this point.

At a seminar, an instructor pulled out a jar and asked the students how many rocks could fit inside. After filling it up with rocks, he asked if it was full. It may have appeared so, but then he poured in gravel. Apparently, the jar was not *completely* full the first time. And while the jar indeed looked full at this point, the instructor was still able to pour in a cup of sand.[35]

The point is that you must fill your day with the most important tasks first, and then let less important tasks fill in the margins. If you fill your jar with sand, there will be no room for a large rock.

---

[35] Stephen R. Covey, A. Roger Merrill and Rebecca R. Merrill, First Things First, 1994: p. 88-89.

Personnel actions are like the sand. If you sit at your desk handling them as they come in, they will fill up your entire day. It's better to get away from your desk during the day, and deliberately attack personnel actions either early in the morning or after the duty day.

Conclusion

This chapter focused on the commander's administrative requirements that relate to personnel. In the next chapter, we'll look at what requirements are required to care for property.

The following documents for this chapter are available online:

1. Example Leave Request SOP

2. Example Pass Request SOP

View available documents at: asktop.net/mocc

Password: 88YEZX9

RESOURCE MANAGER

"Logistics is tough. If it were easy it would be called operations."
—A tired brigade S4[1]

Government employees are charged to "properly use, care for, and safeguard all government property," to "seek [the] most efficient and economical means of accomplishing assigned tasks," and to "limit requests for and use of material to the minimum essential."[2]

"Getting the job done" is a lot easier when you have infinite resources. The challenge, of course, is in choosing how to allocate limited resources among numerous competing priorities. In order to eliminate waste and maximize unit potential, company commanders must establish systems of controls to prevent property loss, eliminate unnecessary monetary expenditures, and maintain equipment.

---

[1] As quoted in *Great Quotes & Quips for the Military Professional,* edited by Bronston Clough
[2] AR 710-2 §1-4m(3), 28 March 2008

Command Supply Discipline Program

Once you take command, your supply responsibilities shift from *assessing* the property on hand to *maintaining* it. There are six aspects to this:

1. Sub hand receipt holder training
2. Periodic inventories
3. Property allocation
4. Lateral transfers and turn-ins
5. Ordering shortages and updating shortage annexes
6. Key control

The Army's difficulties with supply accountability began shortly after the Global War on Terrorism began. Rather than adhere to standards that were designed for a Cold War-era garrison environment, the Army focused on the more immediate task of winning battles. While this is an entirely appropriate activity for a war zone (to say the least), the de-emphasis on property accountability and financial stewardship had a lingering effect.

At the same time, the Army rapidly fielded a number of Commercial Off-The-Shelf (COTS) products. These products may have met the demands of the battlefield, but as time went on, they were difficult to secure replacement parts for and slow to be recalled.

How does the Army fix this problem? It starts with you, and your ability to impose property accountability within your formation. The Army can update regulations, develop new software, and claim that higher level commanders are responsible[3], but these measures will continue to be ineffective until <u>your</u> unit's organizational culture changes.

---

[3] ALARACT 210/2010-EXORD 259-10, Campaign on Property Accountability

Sub-Hand Receipt Holder Training

A strong and firm approach to supply accountability must be balanced with training for soldiers to meet those standards. Given the lack of command emphasis on supply accountability for such a long time, it should not be surprising if your sub-hand receipt holders require training on how to properly manage property.

The first step is to counsel each sub-hand receipt holder on your expectations of them.

During the counseling session, give each sub-hand receipt holder a binder to hold all the materials relating to their property, with the following materials in it:

1. The counseling, along with the excerpts from the relevant regulations
2. Cyclic Schedule from the PBO
3. The signed sub-hand receipt
4. Component hand receipts
5. Shortage annexes, initialed by you
6. The COEI/BII portions of all relevant technical manuals.
7. A CD/DVD with the digital version of all the documents (for their own sub-hand receipts)

Be sure to involve your supply sergeant in compiling these.

Sub-hand receipt holders should then add the following to their binders:

1. Counseling statements given to soldiers assigning them responsibility for equipment
2. DA Form 2062s issuing the property to the user level
3. The signed sub-hand receipt, with notes about who owns it at the user-level
4. Component hand receipts (signed by users)

Inspect these binders regularly, and counsel sub-hand receipt holders who do not meet standards.

As a sub-hand receipt holder prepares to leave the unit, assign a new sub-hand receipt holder to assume responsibilities (in overseas locations, 45 days before DEROS is ideal). If the position will to be vacant due to a personnel gap, a temporary hand receipt holder may be necessary (talk with the first sergeant and supply sergeant about this).

Be sure to brief the new hand receipt holder on your standards, and administer the same counseling you gave their predecessor. If the old sub-hand receipt holder cannot be physically present the "continuity" binder to the new one, have them turn it in to the supply sergeant.

In the past, a Financial Liability Investigation of Property Loss (FLIPL) meant initiating a flag. However, changes to regulations in 2016 eliminated this requirement.[4] While this is a relief to company commanders overseas (whose DEROS would be affected by an end-of-command FLIPL), it limits the control you have over your soldiers. Before a soldier leaves the unit, ensure they conduct a full inventory of their equipment (sub-hand receipt and personal gear) with enough time to process any FLIPL that may be required.

Periodic Inventories

Although regulation permits semi-annual and quarterly inventories, most units adhere to a 10 percent monthly schedule, plus all sensitive items. This includes radios, night vision devices, controlled cryptographic items (CCI), weapons, and ammunition. (In the days before automated reports, CCI and night vision goggles could be done quarterly, but property book officers have since found it easier to have all sensitive items

---

[4] AR 600-8-2 §2-2a, 11 May 2016

inventoried every month.[5] There is also a requirement to inventory tool rooms semi-annually[6].

The trick to efficient and effective cyclic inventories is planning. This is discussed more in Chapter 9, but cyclic inventory planning should be done far enough out to be included in the training calendars. If the operations temp precludes this, you should at least provide the schedule to the first sergeant before the next month's duty rosters are due. The process works like this:[7]

1. Identify what items will be in the upcoming cyclic inventory.
2. Decide which LINs to inventory by like-item (Method 1) and which should be done by sub-hand receipt holder (Method 2).
3. Decide the day, time, and location for each of your sub-hand receipt holders to have their items ready. (Give soldiers plenty of time to find any "temporarily misplaced" tools.
4. Give the schedule to the first sergeant and executive officer. The first sergeant notifies the sub-hand receipt holders and they should tell their subordinate, user-level hand receipt holders. The XO works to ensure like-items are laid out uniformly for quick inspection and technical manuals are on-hand.
5. The supply sergeant or supply clerk should be on hand to record missing or unserviceable items. Missing items must be documented with either a 2062 or a maintenance work order. Also, when conducting like-item inventories, don't release the first soldier until the last soldier is finished.
6. Once the process is complete, have the supply sergeant draw up relief documents for your review no later than the close of business. Don't let the sun go down on property accountability issues.

---

[5] DA PAM 710-2-1 §9-9a, 31 December 1997
[6] DA PAM 710-2-1 §9-5, 31 December 1997
[7] The complete process is detailed in DA PAM 710-2-1 §9-6

Units that make full use of the Automated Identification Technology (AIT) system have a much easier time conducting both cyclic and sensitive item inventories. Instead of reading off endless strings of serial numbers, a handheld device scans the bar codes of the items you have on hand. It's not only convenient, it's what the Army has mandated for all logistics transactions from cradle to grave.[8] If your unit does not have the system up and running, contact the local Sustainment Automation Support Management Office (SASMO). Unlike S-6 channels, SASMO shops specialize in Army software and systems.

Sensitive Item Inventories work similarly:

1. Determine a roster at least two months out and notify the appointed personnel. The appointed personnel must be at least an E-5, though local policies may require a higher rank.[9]

2. Once you receive the sensitive item inventory paperwork from the property book officer, counsel the appointed person on expectations, give them the printout of the items to inventory, and provide them with the unit asset visibility report so they can contact the sub-hand receipt holders.

3. In the counseling, be sure to set a deadline for completion, emphasize the need to check each item for completeness[10], and require that the inventorying officer or NCO write the location for each item (effective for dealing with radios, CAISIs, and other equipment not held in the arms room).

4. Once the inventory is complete, complete Section IV of the counseling appropriately and report the results of the inventory on a memorandum or automated listing to the PBO.[11]

[8] AR 710-2 §1-4d, 28 March 2008
[9] DA PAM 710-2-1 §9-10b, 31 December 1997.
[10] DA PAM 710-2-1 §9-9d(4), 31 December 1997
[11] DA PAM 710-2-1 §9-10b(4), 31 December 1997

How to Handle Lost or Damaged Equipment

For soldiers with damaged or lost items, there are three options. If the soldier admits liability for the loss or damage of a non-controlled item and the value is less than a month's base pay, the soldier can pay for the full value of the loss. (Have the supply sergeant fill out a DD Form 362.) Remember that different categories of items depreciate differently, and that the fair market value for office automation (like computers) can vary greatly from the book value.[12]

If the soldier does not admit liability, the item is controlled, or the item is worth more than one month's base pay, a DD Form 200 needs to be initiated, and you should notify the battalion commander. Depending on the nature of the loss, a FLIPL or AR 15-6 investigation may be initiated, and an investigating officer (SFC or above) may be appointed to look into the matter. (Depending on the amount of evidence immediately available, a "short FLIPL" may be possible.)[13]

To help build a culture of property accountability in your unit, include technical manuals in your sub-hand receipts. Write a serial number on the front so you know whose is whose. The dollar value may be zero, but soldiers who lose them (or keep only the PMCS section) are wasting Army money. A statement of charges may not be possible, but having negligent soldiers carry around a thick book for a week as corrective training may remedy the problem.

In FLIPLs, there are two kinds of liability limits. Findings of simple negligence will lead to an assessment of liability on the soldier up to one month's base pay. Simple negligence is defined as "the absence of due

---

[12] AR 735-5, §B-2, 28 February 2005
[13] AR 735-5, §13-22, 28 February 2005. See the flowchart in Figure 13-10 for the full process.

care, by an act or omission of a person which lacks that degree care for the property that a reasonably prudent person would have taken under similar circumstances, to avoid the loss/damage/destruction of government property."[14]

Gross negligence is a different matter. Defined as "an extreme departure from due care resulting from an act or omission of a person accountable or responsible for Government property which falls far short of that degree of care for the property that a reasonably prudent person would have taken," it is characterized by "a reckless, deliberate, or wanton disregard for the foreseeable loss or damage to the property."[15] Those determined to have displayed gross negligence will be held financially liable for the full amount of the loss/damage/destruction of the equipment.

Other situations may also result in the soldier being held liable for the full amount of the loss. If a soldier loses public funds or personal arms and equipment (PA&E), such as their assigned weapon or organizational clothing and equipment, the full amount may be charged. [16] This clause is designed to prevent soldiers from selling their personal gear; if only a month's base pay were charged, a soldier might profit from such a sale.

A third option exists to adjust losses for up to $100 worth of durable hand tools when negligence or willful misconduct is not suspected.[17] This is most appropriate for tools that are unserviceable through no fault of the soldier. There is a common misperception that commanders can write off "field losses," but this no longer the case under current regulations.

The Army needs to rebuild its culture of supply accountability, and this is best done by establishing high standards early in your command and training soldiers to meet those standards. If a soldier is missing a lock, initiate a statement of charges. A soldier who has to pay $5 for a lock will

---

[14] AR 735-5 §13-29b(2), 28 February 2005.
[15] AR 735-5 §13-29b(3), 28 February 2005.
[16] AR 735-5 §13-41a(6). 28 February 2005. See also §12-1b(2)
[17] AR 735-5 §14-19a, 28 February 2005

understand that you are indeed serious about property accountability, and will be less likely to lose something of greater value.

In addition, remember that part of your command responsibility for property is "taking administrative or disciplinary measures" to safeguard government property.[18] You have the right to issue reprimands, make remarks in evaluation reports, and even recommend bars to continued service.[19] Wield this authority wisely, but use it to both shape your unit's attitude on property accountability and to avoid frivolous FLIPLs.

Property Allocation

As you conducted the change of command inventory, you may have noticed that some sub-hand receipts don't match up exactly with the MTOE paragraphs. For example, MTOEs assign weapons to each section, but the unit armorer signs the hand receipt and controls the items until they are issued. This is normal.

However, now that you are in a position to direct property realignment, you should look again at how equipment is assigned to see if everything makes sense. Print out all sub-hand receipts, comparing each one against the MTOE paragraph. If there is a difference, find out why. If no one can answer, redirect the property to match the MTOE, and ensure any COEI/BII goes with it. The transfer can be done with a DA Form 2062, and easily transferred in the supply system.

To ensure you have an accurate picture of your unit's inventory status, require that the supply sergeant conduct unit level reconciliation reports on a weekly, or at least monthly, basis. This will ensure no equipment is duplicated and nothing remains on your books that has already been turned in.

---

[18] AR 735-5 §2-8a(1)(d), 28 February 2005.
[19] AR 735-5 §12-1a(2), 28 February 2005.

Repeat this process whenever MTOE updates are available in FMSWeb. New items may be added, and others removed or reduced through these changes. Units may request or turn in items within 365 days of the effective date of the new MTOE, so act early and notify which sub-hand receipt holders will be affected.

> Make sure all inventory paperwork is done correctly so no one has an issue during the next change of command inventory. With all luck, that one will be all yours.

Lateral Transfers and Turn-ins

Throughout your command, you will receive lateral transfer directives of equipment to or from other units. Be sure to address these transfers with your supply sergeant quickly, rather than waiting for the suspense date to pass before thinking of it.

The required condition of the equipment is key. Outgoing equipment that must meet "10/20 Standards" requires the equipment to be fully mission capable (FMC) with all COEI/BII. If it does not, your unit may be asked to transfer funds to cover missing items. "Fully Mission Capable plus Safety" is a lower bar, and typically used for excess/obsolete equipment turn-ins or equipment that *must* be transferred (e.g. when a unit is disbanding). Regardless of the transfer/turn-in standard, addressing faults early will allow you to meet deadlines.

From time to time, you may receive lateral transfer directives that simply make no sense (I once received one to turn in a single bayonet). In these cases, prepare a reclama memorandum and send it to the property book officer and S4. Follow up to ensure the directive is cancelled so that you do not attract undue attention in a command and staff meeting.

Ordering Shortages and Updating Shortage Annexes

If your company didn't have 100 percent of its required COEI and BII when you took command, you should spend your time in command to gradually fill those shortages. There are several ways to do this, but they all begin by identifying which items are most essential to the mission and drawing up an "order of merit" list.

Excess and obsolete equipment should be turned in; to do this, request disposition instructions from the property book officer. Order BII for these items only if the lateral transfer instructions require it. For vehicles and other common items, check with the S3 to see if an "Operation Clean Sweep" is coming up soon. These events are excellent opportunities to fill your COEI and BII shortages. Check also with neighboring units—just because a unit is not participating in a Clean Sweep does not mean they don't have excess BII.

For commercial equipment (typically items acquired during the Global War on Terrorism) replacing components can be difficult. Non-standard LINs and components without listed NSNs can make reordering shortages impossible. For these situations, contact the field service representatives (FSRs). This may be a situation where equipment has lingered at the unit because the FSRs weren't aware the item was still on hand. If a newer version of an item is available, it may be worth ordering a new one rather than trying to find parts for the old.

If nothing else, there's always the mission funds account (also called the Operations and Maintenance account). Every battalion is given an annual budget which is used to order supplies and maintenance parts. These orders, summarized in the daily "ZPARK" report, are typically reviewed by the S4 and approved by the battalion executive officer.

Ordering BII shortages with mission funds requires a balanced approach. Order too much at one time and you'll draw unwanted attention. Order too little, and you may not fill as many shortages as you need. Be sure to understand your boss's position—filling shortages is good, but frivolously spending the battalion's mission funds on common types of BII may undermine their confidence in your judgment.

If, for any reason, you are constrained from ordering necessary items, you must draw up a memorandum and report to the next higher command.[20]

Key Control

Physical security of assigned property requires strict control of keys used to access containers, vehicles, and real property. To this end, an appointed key custodian is required to 1) issue and receive keys to and from individuals, 2) maintain an accurate register of all the unit's keys and locks, and 3) investigate and replace lost/stolen keys or locks. To prevent conflicts of interest, key custodians may not be on the unaccompanied access roster for the arms room or serve as either the primary or alternate armorer.[21] Because of this requirement, and the need to investigate losses and assign liability through commander's inquiries, the primary key custodian should be a lieutenant or senior NCO.

After counseling the primary and alternate key custodians on their job duties and appointing them in writing, the first task is to inventory all keys and locks within the unit area, including the motor pool, the company headquarters, and he arms room. (Barracks rooms may be separate.) The key custodian(s) must record the owner, location, and serial number of each key and lock; if a key or lock does not have a serial number, it will have to be inscribed with one.[22] For locks that have multiple key holders, record each person who has a key. The list of all keys, their locations, and the serial numbers must be kept in an authorized key control box.[23]

---

[20] AR 710-2 §1-9, 28 March 2008
[21] AR 190-11 §3-8l, 5 September 2013
[22] AR 190-11 §3-8n, 5 September 2013
[23] AR 190-51 D-6d, 30 September 1993

> To ensure no one removes a lock without authorization, limit access to bolt cutters to two people—you and the primary key custodian. No lock should be cut unless there's someone to sign the statement of charges.

If the unit does not have a key control box, order one through the supply system. Any General Services Administration-approved security container of at least 20-gauge steel is acceptable.[24] There should be two keys to the key control box; one goes to the key custodian, while the other stays with you. If the primary key custodian goes on leave, they must hand their key to their alternate.

At this point, have each key holder sign the DA Form 5513 (Key Control Register and Inventory) and a counseling statement assuming direct responsibility for their locks. Locks for which no one has any keys should be removed and new locks put in place, with the unissued keys kept in the key control box. The DA Form 5513 must be stored in the key control box as well.[25]

Once responsibility has been assigned for all keys and locks, the key custodian should draw up standing operating procedures (SOP) for key holders. At a minimum, the SOP should address what the key custodian's responsibilities are, what the key holders should do if they leave the area (i.e. for TDY or leave), what happens if a key holder fails to turn in a key and is unavailable (statement of charges), and what additional steps key holders must do to out-process the unit. It should also state the requirement for key custodians to conduct a semi-annual inventory.[26]

The end state for key control is a full accounting of all locks and keys, backed up by a system that discourages waste and assigns penalties to

---

[24] AR 190-11 §3-8h, 5 September 2013. This supersedes the 26-gauge steel specified in AR 190-51 D-4, 30 September 1993
[25] AR 190-51 D-3 30 September 1993
[26] AR 190-11 §3-8n, 5 September 2013

careless key holders. Strict adherence to this final element of the supply discipline program is vital for the message it sends—if you won't hesitate to charge someone for that $5 lock, you certainly won't spare them for losing something bigger.

Managing Money

Army budgeting rules establish different "pots" of money for each type of activity, and it's important to understand the limitations on each account.

- **Mission funds.** These are your unit's primary funds for accomplishing your mission, though they're allocated to battalions rather than to each company. Mission funds are used to buy the supplies and maintenance parts needed to keep your unit "mission capable." Before your supply sergeant or maintenance clerks order something, they should bring you the Commander's Exception Reports for signature. Look these over, because even small typographical errors can result in serious, costly mistakes.

There are few more effective ways to mess up an Army career than to make mistakes with money. As a new commander, be sure to consult with the JAG office before considering committing any government funds to an event.

- **Morale, Welfare, and Recreation (MWR)** funds are for "the collective benefit of all unit members for off-duty recreational purposes" such as organizational days and other group events. While they may not be used for farewell ceremony gifts, they may be used to purchase unit histories and related materials for presentation to all unit members and new members at the time they join, as well as welcome home celebrations.[27]

---

[27] AR 215-1 §5-13k , 24 September 2010

- **Family Readiness Group (FRG)** funds come in two types—appropriated funds and informal funds. The appropriated funds are budgeted at higher echelons for FRG operations, typically (though not always) for a unit's deployment. These funds are typically used for the FRG's administrative overhead (such as distributing official newsletters). FRG *informal* funds are private funds raised by FRG members to benefit the FRG membership as a whole. Acceptable uses include hosting holiday parties and recognizing members' significant life events (births, welcoming and farewell parties, etc). They may not be used to augment a unit's cup and flower fund, purchase farewell gifts, or provides loans to individuals. An Army organization may raise FRG funds from its own community members—from those who benefit from it—but may not conduct external fundraisers (such selling cookies at an off-post facility).28 For a full explanation of what you can and can't do to raise and spend FRG funds, contact the local Army Community Services office and ask for their Operation R.E.A.D.Y. brief. ACS has an obligation to conduct informational briefings to commanders within 45 days of assuming command.29

- **Other informal funds.** As the commander, you may authorize informal funds for such activities as office coffee, cup and flower, and annual picnics. However, command policy requires that the use of such funds be consistent with the purpose of the fund, it must be consistent with Army values, and you must appoint an individual to be responsible for fund custody, accounting, and documentation.30 Raising money for a cup and flower fund (used to buy farewell gifts) can be particularly problematic. Soldiers may contribute money but not receive a gift, or there may be perceptions of rank-based favoritism. The safest policy is to have personnel fund their own farewell gifts, and have their teammates provide the inscription text. While it may not be the most popular decision, it is certainly the most equitable.

---

28 AR 608-1 §J-3 and §J-7, 13 March 2013
29 AR 608-1 §2-14k, 13 March 2013
30 AR 600-20 §4-20, 6 November 2014

Unfinanced Requests

When spending mission funds to acquire needed equipment is not an option, consider submitting an unfinanced request (UFR). Every headquarters echelon reserves a certain level of funds for unforeseen needs. If those funds remain unspent, the headquarters may make them available near the end of the fiscal year.

Battalion or brigade S4s will have examples of successful requests on file. The key is to state the costs and show how the project's benefits merit consideration. Prepare for these UFR opportunities by soliciting project ideas and drawing up requests far in advance. Assign responsibility to a platoon leader or section head (this is a great project for an enterprising lieutenant), and submit them as soon as the opportunity arises. Everyone loves free money, but not everyone is in a position to successfully pitch the benefits of their ideas.

Command Maintenance Discipline Program

The American taxpayer may supply the Army with the finest equipment available, but without a good maintenance program it will all be for nothing. Maintenance is about regenerating combat power in preparation for any contingency. Given the readiness requirements the Army faces in the post-ARFORGEN environment, establishing a solid maintenance program is no less important than any other aspect of soldier training.

Generally speaking, the goal is for all equipment to meet "the maintenance standard."[31]

Like an engine, your Command Maintenance Discipline Program (CMDP) requires a number of parts working together to be successful—it must be an internal, self-administered program that is implemented on a routine basis.[32] The component aspects of the CMDP include:

---

[31] AR 750-1 §3-2, 12 September 2013
[32] DA PAM 710-1 §10-8, 4 December 2013

1. Driver's training
2. Appointing managers
3. Standing operating procedures
4. Unscheduled maintenance
5. Dispatching vehicles
6. Scheduled maintenance
7. Maintenance meetings
8. Training for operators and maintenance crews

Driver's Training

In order to properly diagnose problems with vehicles, you must have operators who can conduct preventive maintenance checks and services (PMCS) to standard. And since a soldier *must* be licensed before they can legitimately conduct PMCS on a vehicle, conducting PMCS to standard begins with driver's training.[33]

As a company commander, you have three responsibilities: 1.) develop and publish guidance for interviewing and selecting driver candidates, 2.) conduct (or appoint someone to conduct) the driver candidate interviews, and 3.) ensure operators are licensed before operating a vehicle.[34]

The task of driver/operator training, to include testing and licensing, falls to your battalion headquarters.[35] Why? Because battalions can generate economies of scale by pooling resources in ways individual companies cannot. If your battalion lacks an effective driver's training and licensing program, you'll end up with unlicensed and/or untrained junior soldiers and an increased chance of user error.

---

[33] DA PAM 750-1 Figure 4-1, 4 December 2013
[34] AR 600-55 §1-4b, 18 June 2007. See Appendix B for a list of sample questions
[35] AR 600-55 §1-4g(3), 18 June 2007

If your battalion doesn't have an effective driver's training program, ask your battalion commander if it's a command priority. You may have to start your own training program, or at least create company-level 'certification' classes on conducting PMCS. Either way, you'll be using company resources that should be allocated at the battalion level.

One of the required points of instruction for driver's training is PMCS. Your drivers should come out of driver's training with at least a general understanding of what PMCS is and how to do it. After completing the course and passing the driver's test, the driver testing station (or unit) issues an OF 346 with the words "ARMY STANDARD." [36] With the training and a license, an operator may perform PMCS on equipment for which they are certified.

Test your soldiers' PMCS skills regularly, and build teams by testing platoons. An earlier release on Friday (even one hour) builds esprit de corps. The idea of taking the -10 manual home to study it for a quiz the following day should not seem like a strange idea."

To enforce accountability in PMCS, show up an hour early with the first sergeant and check 3 items on each vehicle. After all platoons report that they are finished, dismiss all junior enlisted soldiers and have NCOs stand by their vehicles as you walk around and ask questions.

"What did you find today? Any faults? How were the fluid levels?" You'll find out quickly who knows their equipment and who thought they had better things to do. The latter group are the people who get to stay late.

---

[36] AR 600-55 §6-1d and §6-3b(1), 18 June 2007

Appointing Managers

Trained operators require leadership to direct their efforts, and you won't be able to do this alone. You must appoint personnel to several types of duties in order to monitor all aspects of your CMDP.

First, each level of command requires an appointed logistics readiness officer.[37] In combat arms units, the best candidate is usually the executive officer; in standalone logistics companies, it's the maintenance warrant officer. Whoever you pick, an effective maintenance program requires the maintenance manager to know the extent of their responsibilities[38] and be trained how to accomplish them.

Logistics readiness officer training is available from the installation or division G4 through a Maintenance Assistance and Instruction Team (MAIT) Program.[39] The MAIT program offers courses for executive officers, battalion-level maintenance managers, and publications managers. They may also offer courses on the Army Records Information Management System (ARIMS), the Global Combat Support System (GCSS), and how to handle Test, Measurement, & Diagnostic Equipment (TMDE).

Second, you must appoint personnel who can address specific maintenance programs. With the advice of the maintenance manager and the first sergeant, select support coordinators for TMDE[40], Warranties[41], Corrosion Prevention[42], Modification Work Orders (MWOs)[43], and the Army Oil Analysis Program (AOAP).[44] In addition, appoint a primary and alternate dispatcher, and provide a DA Form 1687 signature card for mechanics to pick up maintenance parts. [45]

---

[37] AR 750-1 §2-20t,12 September 2013
[38] See AR 700-138 §1-18d, 26 February 2004
[39] AR 750-1 §8-15b, 12 September 2013
[40] AR 750-43 §2-10, 24 January 2014
[41] AR 700-139 §1-11d(7), 2 February 2015
[42] AR 750-59 §2-9 and §2-10, 19 March 2014
[43] AR 750-10 §2-16, 5 August 2013
[44] AR 750-1 §2-19q and §8-2b(4), 12 September 2013
[45] DA Pam 750-8 §2-2 and §1-9a(6)(d), 22 August 2005

Once personnel receive training for their jobs (either from a MAIT course or the battalion maintenance officer), have them develop standing operating procedures (SOP) to govern all aspects of maintenance operations.[46] In addition to the topics discussed in this section, it should assign responsibility for both operators and mechanics, as well as roles for The Army Maintenance Management System (TAMMS) procedures from AR 750-8. Counsel the logistics readiness officer that the team has 30 days to develop the SOP based on the battalion's version, and check in on their progress weekly.

Performing Unscheduled Maintenance

The purpose of command maintenance on the first day of the week is to identify vehicle faults. The goal is to correct them quickly so that your unit's equipment readiness is not impacted. With maintenance leaders who understand their responsibilities and trained operators who know how to do perform PMCS properly, unscheduled maintenance is significantly more effective. In a sense, "unscheduled maintenance" is a bit of a misnomer—it's a vital element to include in the training schedule.

Sub-hand receipt holders should sign for TMs just like other BII, and ensure operators are responsible for them. If an operator loses their TM, note the soldier's name and section. Instead of a statement of charges (for something that's officially zero dollars), give corrective training by requiring the soldier to carry around a large book or binder for a few days.

The most successful units approach command maintenance methodically. At the initial accountability formation, one of the maintenance leaders speaks about a common problem, with then operators then

---

[46] AR 750-1 §3-7b, 12 September 2013

gathering around one or more vehicles to see what "right" looks like. The lesson is rehearsed and takes roughly 10 minutes.

The unit distributes the pre-printed DA Form 5988-Es to platoons, who then pass them to operators (no one is left standing around). Each operator has the correct technical manual (TM) for their vehicle, and each operator—no matter how many times they've done it—goes through it, step by step.

Have your full gear available for PMCS. Crawl underneath vehicles with your operators. The first time you do it, the first sergeant will be able to hear a pin drop—nine times out of ten, your soldiers will have never seen an officer do that before.

Operators record faults according to steps in the TM (not 1, 2, 3…) and mark whether or not the fault is a "deadline-able" one. When complete, the operator turns in the 5988-E to their supervisor, who reviews and checks for accuracy. If correct, the supervisor turns it in to the platoon sergeant (or the platoon's maintenance representative).

By noon, the platoon sergeant will have received the 5998-Es for all of the rolling stock and turned them in to maintenance for processing.

Monday afternoon is reserved for fault verification of vehicles and PMCS on a rotational weekly subject—communications equipment, weapons, CBRN equipment, or generators. Operators whose vehicles have faults need to meet with the quality assurance and control mechanics who then verify faults. If the fault is confirmed, the maintenance clerk records the fault and checks to see if parts are hand to correct the fault (from "bench stock").

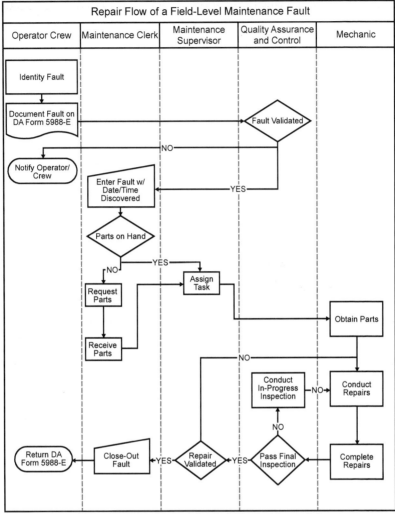

Repair Flow of a Field-Level Maintenance Fault				
Operator Crew	Maintenance Clerk	Maintenance Supervisor	Quality Assurance and Control	Mechanic

Identity Fault

Document Fault on DA Form 5988-E

Fault Validated

NO

Notify Operator/ Crew

Enter Fault w/ Date/Time Discovered

YES

Parts on Hand

NO

YES

Assign Task

Request Parts

Obtain Parts

Receive Parts

NO

Conduct In-Progress Inspection

NO

Conduct Repairs

NO

Return DA Form 5988-E

Close-Out Fault

YES

Repair Validated

YES

Pass Final Inspection

YES

Complete Repairs

DA Pam 750-1 Figure 3-1. Repair flow of a field-level maintenance fault

Have each operator/crew keep printouts of DA Pam 750-1 Figures 3-1 and 4-1 in their binders. If there's a fault on their vehicle, they should know exactly who to contact.

If the parts are not on hand, the clerk orders them. If they are, the maintenance supervisor assigns the task to the appropriate level for application.

For example, a windshield wiper blade can be applied by an operator. Replacing a headlight may require a mechanic. (To prevent arguments between maintenance and platoon leadership, detail in the SOP what kinds of repairs are "operator level.")

This sets the stage for Tuesday morning, when mechanics perform the unscheduled maintenance that is beyond operators' normal skill sets. The equipment's operators are not excused. They are there to assist the mechanics and validate that the equipment is serviceable once repairs are finished.

Ideally, by the close of business on Monday you should know which pieces of equipment were FMC, which ones had correctable faults, and which ones had faults that will require mechanics to work on them. (This will allow you to prioritize repairs.)

By noon on Tuesday, any vehicles that still have deadline-able faults are considered non-mission capable (NMC). For quick reference, you can have the logistics readiness officer prepare a one-page Excel spread-sheet that shows the readiness status of each type of equipment (called a "combat slant").

FMC equipment is available for dispatch.

By regulation, the signature of the commander's designated repre-sentative is sufficient to authorize dispatches.[47] However, individual battalion practices vary widely. A unit may have the company com-mander sign for on-post dispatches, with the battalion commander authorizing off-post movements. Check the battalion SOP for guidance.

---

[47] As described in the "AUTHORIZATION" paragraph in DA PAM 750-8 Figure 2-7, 22 August 2005

Dispatching Vehicles

Before a vehicle leaves the motor pool, it must be properly dispatched according to procedures. The kind of unit you command determines how frequently you'll be called on to sign a dispatch.

| COMBAT SYSTEMS | | | | | |
Model	OH	FMC	NMCS	NMCM	OR
M1126 Stryker ICV	5	4	0	1	80%
M1127 Stryker RV	7	7	0	0	100%
M1129 Stryker MCV	2	2	0	0	100%
M1130 Stryker CV	2	1	1	0	50%
M1133 Stryker MEV	2	2	0	0	100%
TOTAL	18	16	1	1	88%

Non-mission capable equipment is divided in to NMC-Supply and NMC-Maintenance to identify types of constraints

Before authorizing a dispatch, you'll need to check several items on both the DA Form 5987-E Motor Equipment Dispatch and DA form 5988-E Maintenance & Inspection Worksheet.

1. What is the mission, where is it going, and what is the proper authorization level?
2. Are overdue services listed on the 5987-E? A vehicle with overdue services should not be dispatched.
3. Is the operator also the official user listed on the 5987-E? If not, require a DA Form 2062 hand receipt showing the operator has signed for the vehicle along with all COEI/BII from the hand receipt holder. To save time, have operators use the preprinted 2062s available through the Logistics Information Warehouse's ETMs Online application.[48] This will ensure property is accounted for at all times.

---

[48] https://www.logsa.army.mil/etms/index.cfm?fuseaction=viewsearchfo rm&CFID=764206&CFTOKEN c9acd19179307a74-CF237CDB-C4F8-2AEA-05B86692416EC904

4. Do both operators have the equipment listed on their DA Form 5984-E Operator's ID Card? If so, have both sign on the Operator's Signature blanks of the 5987-E. This will allow the second operator to drive if there is an emergency. If not, consider the length of the mission—long missions may necessitate a second qualified driver.

5. Check the DA Form 5988-E to see if there were any faults. If so, were they corrected? If they were not corrected, consider carefully whether to authorize the dispatch.

6. Units may use a Quality Assurance/Quality Check (QA/QC) form to check on operators. If one is required, ensure it is filled out completely, and that the dispatcher is among those listed on your appointment orders.

7. Operators should also have a blank accident form and, if transporting hazardous materials, a material handling sheet for each item. For this, you may also involve the company's HAZMT certifier.

If everything checks out, the paperwork is complete. Sign the Authorization blank.

An inoperable headlight will deadline a vehicle, but doesn't increase risk during a daytime mission. However, if the mission runs late, that same fault becomes much more serious. Be careful when dispatching a vehicle with faults.

Scheduled Maintenance

Successful unscheduled maintenance is a matter of training, procedure, and accountability. Successful *scheduled* maintenance, on the other hand, is a matter of planning.

Your logistics readiness officer should provide you with a calendar of scheduled services. Enter these dates into the training calendar, along with the names of the assigned operators so that they can assist the mechanics. Two months before the scheduled dates, notify the first sergeant so that the operators have no schedule conflicts.

Maintenance Meetings

CMDP requires visibility on your maintenance status, so schedule a formal weekly update to discuss both scheduled and unscheduled services (sometime after the Tuesday noon deadline). This meeting should be chaired by your logistics readiness officer and include platoon leadership. You may also want to have an operations sergeant there to note which operators' schedules will be affected by scheduled services.

One approach is to review the 026 battalion deadline report and have platoon leaders brief their combat slants along with the parts statuses. For example, "Stryker #119 has a broken widget. The part is on order, set to arrive on [date]. That's a two day repair; so we expect it to be FMC by [D+2]." Provide briefers with a Logistician's Cheat Sheet so that they have the supply status codes.

Issues that can be corrected at the company level, such as "Parts Received, Not Installed," can be addressed here, as they can indicate which aspect of the CMDP is having problems. Operators may be absent, out for a school, or not skilled enough to apply the part. Mechanics may be understaffed, on too many details, or incorrectly diagnosing faults. Solicit feedback to identify systemic problems.

Review the field-level maintenance information published in Preventive Maintenance Magazine every month. Sign up for a subscription and maintain a set on hand for three years so that operators, maintainers, and clerks have ready access to important topics.[49]

Look for issues that can be corrected by higher levels, such as long backorder times on parts or extensive repairs that can be handled by a higher echelon. Also, listen for job orders that will require coordination with the maintenance company's specialty shops. For instance, quarterly

---

[49] DA Pam 750-3 §3-7, 18 September 2013

services for weapons systems are beyond a unit armorer's skills set; these must be done by 91F Small Arms Repairers.

In addition, pay attention for issues that can be corrected by controlled exchange or even cannibalization. These situations require a very specific set of conditions to be appropriate, one of which is approval by the O-5 commander or sustainment maintenance commander.[50] Nevertheless, these are options that should be considered given the right circumstances merit consideration.

Periodically, review the condition of transportation containers, eligibility for driver/mechanic badges,[51] and the status of recoverable "exchange parts." These parts are sold to the Army by vendors at a discounted rate on the condition that old parts will be returned after use. To reduce waste, make sure that these parts are tracked and returned in a timely manner.

When conducted properly, maintenance meetings provide not only visibility to multiple subordinate levels on what *is happening*, but also accountability for those levels on what *should have happened*. If you can't attend every meeting, be sure to attend them at least *regularly*. Have some questions ready, but mostly just sit back and listen. These meetings should serve as training opportunities, but can also provide you with material for subordinates' evaluations.

Arms Room

No one aspect of company operations involves as many appointed duties and staff proponents as the arms room. The primary and alternate armorers, the supply sergeant, the logistics readiness officer, the key custodian, the physical security officer, maintenance, and the S4 all have an interest in making sure there are no issues with arms room operations.

---

[50] AR 7101 §4-9 (Controlled Exchange) and §4-10 (Cannibalization), 12 September 2013.
[51] AR 600-8-22 §8-31, 11 December 2006

Appointment Orders

The first step is to appoint the armorers. Assuming there are no character issues, the most natural choice is the 92Y10 supply specialist. Every 92Y receives unit armorer training as part of their Advanced Individual Training (AIT), and most units have the position. For the same reasons, appoint the supply sergeant as the alternate armorer. Additional assistant armorers can be chosen and sent to training based on needs. Screen and evaluate personnel using DA Form 7281, and contact the local provost marshal for the mandatory background checks.[52]

> Have the supply sergeant sign the sub-hand receipt for the arms room, and let them further sub-hand receipt to their supply clerk as the primary armorer. As the alternate armorer and the supply clerk's supervisor, the supply sergeant will be "involved." As a hand receipt holder, they'll be "invested."

Next, develop the accompanied and unaccompanied access rosters to post inside the arms room.[53] The unaccompanied access roster should list only those who have responsibility for property—you and the two armorers. The accompanied list should include the physical security officer, the first sergeant, the logistics readiness officer, any assistant armorers, and the sensitive item inventory officer for that month.

The armorer's first job is to develop the Master Authorization List (MAL)— the list of every weapon and to whom it's assigned. Ensure the armorer updates this monthly using a AAA-162 from the Orderly Room. With the MAL, the armorer can generate the DA Form 3749 Equipment Receipts showing which weapons a soldier is authorized to draw. You will have to sign these before they can be laminated and distributed.

---

[52] AR 190-11 §2-11, 5 September 2013
[53] AR 190-11 §4-19a, 5 September 2013

Drawing Weapons

Ensure the armorers understand unit standards for drawing weapons. Ranges and other issuances for less than 24 hours require only the turn in of the 3749. For field exercises or periods longer than 24 hours, soldiers must not only turn in the 3749, but also make an entry onto the control sheet/log.[54]

Some installations have a form for this; if yours does not, pre-print DA Form 2062s that list each weapon system's BII and keep these near the armory door. As a soldier enters the arms room, they fill out the 2062 with their name and their weapon's serial number (from the 3749). When the soldier reaches the counter, they turn in their 3749 and the signed 2062, then receive their weapon with its BII.

Privately owned weapons and ammunition may be stored in the arms room. Like government weapons, owners will require a DA Form 3749, and weapons must be inventoried monthly.[55]

Maintenance

Weapons must receive PMCS at least monthly, either by the armorer or their assigned owners. If the armorer is responsible, make sure they are getting the necessary 5988-Es to record the results. Copies should be kept in both the arms room and the maintenance office.

Because unit armorers are technically performing an additional duty, rather than an official MOS, they should only be responsible for inspection, disassembly, assembly, physical security, and operator level maintenance of unit weapons. They are not authorized to perform field level maintenance on weapons.

Field level maintenance is the responsibility of the 91F Small Arms Repairer found in dedicated maintenance companies. For quarterly maintenance, you need to coordinate with a maintenance company.

[54] AR 190-11 §4-19e(3), 5 September 2013
[55] AR 190-11 §4-5d(2)(b), 5 September 2013

Physical Security

The physical security officer (PSO) is appointed at battalion levels and higher, typically from the S2 shop.[56] Because the arms room is a designated "mission essential and vulnerable area" (MEVA), you should request a physical security inspection to determine whether the arms room meets standards or needs corrections, and if key control procedures are being followed.[57] If the battalion PSO is not available, contact the garrison. If the inspection includes a test of the Intrusion Detection System (IDS), be sure to contact the local provost marshal beforehand.[58]

Pilferable high-value items such as watches, compasses, and binoculars should not be stored in the arms room if other facilities are available. However, if this is not possible, draw up a memorandum specifically authorizing storage and keep them in the arms room in a lockable container.[59]

When units share a consolidated arms rooms, installations designate one commander to be a single point of contact. This commander establishes the SOP and assumes overall responsibility for the facility. The SOP should govern all aspect of arms room operations for tenant units, including any requirements to provide armed guards in the event of an IDS failure.[60]

Command Deployment Discipline Program

Supply and maintenance clearly have significant roles in the day-to-day rhythm of company operations, but all the readiness in the world will mean nothing if you cannot deploy your unit. The Command Deployment Discipline Program (CDDP) addresses this increasingly important capability.

---

[56] AR 190-13 §3-1a, 25 February 2011
[57] AR 190-13 §1-24c and §2-7c(1), 25 February 2011
[58] See AR 190-13 §9-2, 25 February 2011, for details about required signage
[59] AR 190-11 §4-18b, 5 September 2013
[60] AR 190-11 §4-4f, 5 September 2013

There are five parts to a good CDDP:

1. Appointments
2. Training
3. OEL/Movement Plan development
4. Container management
5. Inspections

Appointments

First, appoint personnel for the required additional duties, including Unit Movement Officers (UMOs), Hazardous Materials (HAZMAT) certifiers, Container Control Officers (CCOs), and air load planners. [61] Depending on the installation, rail teams may also be required.

UMOs bear overall responsibility for deployment planning. They operate the deployment planning software, prepare and maintain unit movement plans, develop and update the Organizational Equipment List (OEL), and—once notified of a deployment—create the Unit Deployment List. The primary UMO must have a secret security clearance and must be E6 or above[62], but rank should not be the only consideration. Lieutenants, for example, have shown to be poor choices for UMOs because of their inexperience and potential for frequent turnover.[63]

> Supply and maintenance clearly have significant roles in the day-to-day rhythm of company operations, but all the readiness in the world will mean nothing if you cannot deploy your unit.

The primary and alternate HAZMAT certifiers are responsible for making safe—but efficient—use of shipping containers. Certain types of hazardous materials, such as lithium batteries, are safe when stored in their

---

[61] AR 525-93, §2-17x(18), 12 November 2014
[62] AR 525-93, Table C-1, 12 November 2014
[63] http://www.alu.army.mil/alog/issues/JulAug06/umo_tcamis.html

proper containers. Others are extremely volatile, and may not exceed certain quantities or be mixed with other substances when transported. The HAZMAT certifier checks on the UMO's deployment plans to ensure each HAZMAT will be stored properly; to prevent conflict of interest, the sane person may not hold both duties.[64]

Air load planners are required for designing load plans and to lead teams in building pallets for air movements. For companies that deploy independently of their parent battalions, the air load planner works with the brigade mobility officer, Logistics Readiness Center and the Air Force to prepare equipment for transport.

Container control officers are responsible for checking the serviceability of transportation containers, and must be an E-6 or higher.[65] Involve maintenance personnel with this duty—there is frequently a need to estimate container repair times and costs.

Training

UMOs, as the principal coordinators for movements, must be trained not only on the on the Unit Movement Officer's Deployment Planning Course, but also the Transportation Coordinators' Automated Information for Management System II (TC-AIMS II) software.[66] Course information will be available through the S3 Schools point of contact.

HAZMAT certifiers must pass an 80-hour course to be certified. Course topics include air, land, and ocean transportation and storage of hazardous materials, including ammunition. HAZMAT certifiers are also valuable assets in garrison when determining what storage requirements the motor pool needs to safely store petroleum, oil, and lubricants (POL).

---

[64] AR 525-93 §2-17x(12), 12 November 2014
[65] AR 56-4 §1-4k(7), 17 September 2014
[66] AR 525-93 §4-9b(2), 12 November 2014

Container control is an online course, found on the Army Training Requirements and Resources System (ATRRS) website as the "Intermodal Dry Cargo CNTR/CSC Reinspection" course. Because of this, the CCO will likely require additional, real-life experience to be proficient. (The best resources for experts are the 88N Movement Coordinators found in logistics battalions and movement control teams.) The software for container management is officially the Integrated Booking System/Container Management Module,[67] but the older system, the Army Container Asset Management System (ACAMS), is still in use because of the more detailed information it can provide. CCOs are required to have a valid ACAMS account.[68]

Air load planners require training in the iCodes software. For this and any required rail team training, refer to the battalion's S3 Schools point of contact.

Organization Equipment List/Movement Plan Development

"In preparing for battle I have always found that plans are useless, but planning is indispensable."—GEN Dwight D. Eisenhower

The OEL is the full list of the company's personnel and equipment. Once the UMO is fully trained, they can enter required relevant data into the deployment software (e.g. TC-AIMS) using a AAA-162 and the property book. This should be updated quarterly.

The Unit Deployment List (UDL) is derived from the OEL, and consists only of personnel and equipment that will be going on the deployment. During the Global War on Terrorism, units frequently left behind equipment and fell in on theater-provided equipment already in-country. UDLs will be much smaller than OELs if the property book will be split and there are rear detachment personnel.

---

[67] AR 56-4 §3-5d(1), 17 September 2014
[68] AR 56-4 B-4c, 17 September 2014

The UDL is only developed when the unit receives a movement order, but the UMO can develop a movement plan far in advance. It should address such subjects as how the unit will muster, prepare air load pallets, and move personnel and equipment to the point of embarkation.

Container Management

Container management is a large-scale project. The goal is to repair unserviceable containers, reduce the unit's container footprint, create 20-foot equivalent containers, and certify good containers for shipment. However, a frequent problem is that containers are used for storage and serviceability is ignored. This is a serious impediment to deployment readiness.

To start, the container control officer should conduct a survey of all containers in the unit's footprint, and note deficiencies on a DA Form 2404s (the old, "analog" version of the 5988-E). Punctures, dents, bends and rusted areas are deficiencies that are best corrected by a maintenance company because of it's organic welding team. Damage that affects the container's structural integrity may require evacuation, or—in severe cases—may be irreparable.

Next, inventory all containers that you haven't already looked through during the change of command. Many times, commanders do not realize what's inside these containers because they don't appear on the property book, or there's nothing on the property book inside. Nevertheless, in order to repair a container it will have to be emptied, which means turning in excess and condensing container usage. Once a container is repaired and returned, fill it only with necessary equipment, draw up a load plan, and list its contents on a DA Form 1750 to be posted inside the door.

Finally, certify serviceable containers, and develop a schedule to have them recertified every two years. Maritime shipping has two standards for containers—one for shipping ammunition and another, less stringent one for general cargo. You should have enough of the International Maritime Dangerous Goods (IMDG) code containers to transport your basic load.

Even if you can't get enough empty containers, you can develop load plans ahead of time by marking off the container dimensions on the ground and laying equipment out within the boundaries. It's not perfect, but it's better than waiting until the last minute, and it's extremely cost effective.

Once this process is complete, empty containers that cannot be economically repaired should be turned in for scrap and removed from the property book.

Inspections

CDDP evaluations will include a review of the OEL, movement plans, load teams, and the status of additional duties. Unit commanders typically request the informal inspections—staff assistance visits and courtesy inspections before a formal inspection. Formal inspections are either included in the Command Inspection Program or performed separately. Regardless, the best way to prepare for an inspection is to fulfill all the requirements listed in AR 525-93 Figure C-1.

Pursuing Excellence

Whether or not you're confident in your supply, maintenance, or deployment programs, competing for an excellence award will only make your unit better, and distinguish it from others. If you want to pursue either the Supply Excellence Award (SEA), Army Award for Maintenance Excellence (AAME), or Deployment Excellence award (DEA), ask the S4 about the timelines for each, then approach your battalion commander about wanting to compete. If you do this early in your command, you're more likely to have enough time to prepare and have a successful candidacy.

If the battalion commander supports you, assign responsibility, discuss expectations, and schedule internal inspections monthly according to the regulatory checklists.[69] Request quarterly staff assistance visits to make sure you're on track, put together your packet well in advance, and solicit input from higher level staff proponents.

Conclusion

Property management is the quantifiable way to prove to your boss that you know what you're doing, but it's not everything. The Army is still very much a "people business." Knowing how to manage your people is just as important as how to manage materiel.

---

[69] See AR 710-2 Appendix B for the SEA checklist, AR 750-1 Appendix D for the AAME, and AR 525-93 Chapter 5 for the DEA. Note that the DEA requires a deployment, redeployment, or deployment support mission to compete.

Logistics Code Cheat Sheets

SUPPLY STATUS CODES	
BA	Item processed for release
BB	Item back ordered against due in stock
BC	Item back ordered expect long ESD
BD	Request delayed - Need to verify Req's
BE	Depot/storage activity has a record of the MRO
BF	No record of Document Number
BG	One or more items are incorrect
BH	Substitute item will be supplied
BJ	Qty changed to conform to package
BK	Requisition data modified
BL	Notice of availability forwarded to country rep
BM	Document forwarded to activity
BN	Transaction is being processed as a free issue
BP	Requisition deferred per customer instructions
BQ	Cancelled by request (DSU)
BR	Cancelled by activity (Higher)
BS	Cancelled by activity
BT	Requisition received and processed for attempted
BV	Item procured by contract or direct consignee
BZ	Processed for direct delivery
B7	Unit price changed
B9	Cancellation
CA	Rejected
CB	Rejected, quantity not filled as required
CD	Rejected, errors in quantity
CE	Rejected, errors in unit of issue
CG	Rejected, unable to identify requested item
CH	Rejected, sent to incorrect manager
CJ	Rejected, item code obsolete or inactivated
CK	Rejected, item not available, (see DS4)
CL-CZ	Rejected
CS	Rejected, qty ordered is suspect to error
C1-C9	Rejected
D2-D8	Rejected
AOA	Routine request
AE1	Status
AF1	Follow-up
AC1	Request for cancellation

WORK REQUEST STATUS (TABLE B-21)

A	Awaiting Initial Inspection
B	In Shop
C	Awainting Shop
D	Deferred
E	Awating Final Inspection
F	Final Inspection Complete
G	Test flight, or maintenance operational check
H	Awaiting Disposition Instructions from Higher
I	Awaiting Shop While Awaiting non-NMC Parts
J	In Shop Awaiting NMCS Parts
K	Awaiting Non-NMCS Parts
L	Evac NMCS
M	Evac NMCM
N	Evac Depot
O	Awaiting Evacuation
P	NMC for Lack of Facilities/Tools/Test Equipment
Q	Awaiting ECOD Actions
R	Awaiting Pickup
S	Work Complete, Customer Not Notified
T	Closed, Completed by other Maintenance Activity
U	Picked-Up
V	Closed (Item Satisfied ORF Exchange)
W	Work Request Closed (Uneconomically Repair)
X	Work Request Closed (Didn't meet Acceptance)
Y	Closed (Below Acceptance Standard)
Z	Work Order Cancelled
1	Awaiting Deadlining NMCS Parts
6	Re-Inspection (rework the job)
7	Awaiting Float Transaction
8	Rework, return to Shop
9	Begin Intransit Time

LEVEL OF WORK CODES TABLE B-24)

O	Unit/AVUM
F	Direct Support/AVIM
H	General Support
D	Depot
K	Contractor
L	Special Repair Activity

COMMON SUPPLY TERMS

ASA	Same as RFI
ASL	Authorized Stockage List
CRP	Central Receiving Point
D6S	A receipt document
DFG	Dedicated Due-in/due-out
EDD	Estimated Delivery Date
ESD	Estimated Ship Date
ESTB	Requisition Established
MIRP	Date a D6S has been processed
MRO	Material Release Order
NICP	National Inventory Control Point
NRF	No Record Found
O/T	Requisition passed to higher source
PLL	Prescribed Load List
RFI	Released for Issue
SHPD	Shipped from Depot
SSAR	Supply Support Activity Receipt

DEPOTS

A35	New Cumberland, PA
AQ5	Sharp, CA
B16	CECOM
B17	St. Louis, MO
B46	Warrenton, VA
BO7	Rock Island, IL
BA4	Anniston, CA
BK4	Letterkenny, PA
BL6	Lexinton, KY
BP4	Pueblo, CO
BR4	Texarkana, TX
BS2	Corpus Cristi, TX
BS6	Sacramento, CA
SA	Mechanicsburg, PA
SC	Columbus, OH
SM	Memphis, TN
SN	New Cumberland, PA
SR	Richmond, VA
SU	Ogden, UT
S9I	Dayton, OH

ADVICE CODES (Unit Request)

1C	Fill as requested, substitute or reject if item not available
1J	Fill as requested or reject if item not available
2A	Item is not available through manufacturer, fabrication or procurement
2B	Only requested item will suffice, do not substitute
2C	Do not backorder, reject unfilled quantity, suitable substitute acceptable
2D	Furnish exact quantity requested
2E	Free Issue
2F	Item is coded obsolete but still required for immediate use
2G	Multiple use
2H	Special textile requirements
2J	Do not substitute of backorder
2L	The amount shown exceeds normal demand, valid requirement
2T	Deliver to consignee by RDD, or cancel requirement

MODES OF SHIPMENT

A	Motor Transport
B	Motor (less than truckload)
G	Surface Parcel Post
H	Air Parcel Post
I	Government Truck
J	Small Package Carrier
Q	Air Freight/Express/Charter
R	Expedited Air Freight
S	Scheduled Truck Service
5	United Parcel Service (UPS)
6	Military Official Mail
7	Express Mail

The following document for this chapter is available online:

1. Logistics Status Code Cheat Sheets—AP 2.16. Appendix 2.16 Status Codes

2. Logistics Status Code Cheat Sheet (Abridged)

View available documents at: asktop.net/mocc

Password: 88YEZX9

7

CONSCIENCE/COUNSELOR/ COACH

"As a division and lower commander, assume the attitude of that of a 'coach' of your winning team. Use the attitude of the 'commander' very sparingly and only for unusual situations."—General Bruce C. Clarke

What does it mean to "take care of soldiers?" As a company commander, you are more than just a manager or boss. Some of the soldiers in your company may be fresh out of high school and looking to prove themselves in the "real world." Others are away from home for the first time in their lives, and are still deciding who they want to be. Many are earning a paycheck in their first full-time job, but don't know how to manage their money or credit. Given that they are the future of the Army, you owe it to your soldiers, their parents, and the nation to guide them, help them, and mentor them.

Guiding soldiers means providing role models for our youngest generation of soldiers. Every leader in the Army is expected to "set and exemplify the highest ethical and professional standards as embodied in the Army Values."[1] Obviously, this applies to you, but as the unit commander you

---

[1] AR 600-100 §2-1a, 8 March 2007

have a special responsibility: to not only set the standard for behavior in your unit, but to influence other leaders to do the same.

The Army's many programs allow you to leverage your authority through numerous appointed duties. You can't be everywhere at once, but everyone—leaders and soldiers—should be able to use your example to guide their ethical and moral decisions and deter misconduct. Conceptually, you act as the unit's *conscience*.

Yet relying on formal, mandatory programs alone to guide soldiers and other leaders is too mechanical an approach for regular human beings. You need other, more informal methods to effectively help soldiers handle personal issues. Plus, those who make bad choices deserve a chance at rehabilitation. In many ways, you act as a *counselor*.

As the *coach*, you develop a winning team. You promote the unit's successes, and if deterrence and rehabilitation can't turn someone around, make hard decisions about who gets to "still play on the team." You help subordinates achieve professional goals, and as the public face of the unit, lead interactions with outside entities such as the Family Readiness Group.

Army programs often require use of all three approaches. The Army Substance Abuse Program, for example, looks to deter illegal drug use. Offenders get one chance at rehabilitation; if caught a second time they face separation. A good commander knows when to use the roles of the conscience, counselor, and coach to build a disciplined, ready unit with high esprit de corps. But first, they need a solid base of technical knowledge on what each program is and what it's for.

The Safety Program

The purpose of the safety program is to preserve Army resources (including personnel, property, and equipment) against accidental loss. It uses "deliberate risk management" as the primary method to eliminate unnecessary risk and institutes safety investigations as a way to collect lessons learned.

The degree to which safety must be integrated into everyday missions largely depends on what kind of unit you are in. For obvious reasons, safety in an aviation unit will be a much bigger concern than in a finance company. Yet there are a few basics that apply to every unit.

The first step to building a company safety program starts with the Commander's Safety Course, which is available through ALMS and must be completed prior to assuming command.[2] This training will give you a handle on the technical side of the safety program, including the risk management and accident reporting processes. The most important take-away is that every "Army Accident" requires a report, whether it's a $2,000 on-duty convoy fender bender with no injuries, a hamstring pull that lands a soldier in the hospital a one-day quarters profile, or a full-blown off-duty car accident with a fatality.[3]

Next, work with the first sergeant to select a company-level safety officer. This person should be familiar enough with company operations to identify common risks inherent to the unit's training and/or missions, which is usually at least a staff sergeant.[4] As an alternate, select someone living in the barracks who can be trained to identify and report various safety hazards, such as expired fire extinguishers. If one is available, select an E5 so they can also help with accident investigations.

---

[2] AR 385-10 §10-6, 27 November 2013
[3] AR 385-10 §3-4, 27 November 2013 lists the accident class definitions.
[4] DA PAM 685-10 §3-3f, 23 May 2008

British sea captain Thomas Cochrane was just twenty-five and the *Speedy* was his first independent command, but he would go on to terrorize the French by capturing over fifty vessels in the Mediterranean and harassing French troops in raids on the coasts of France and French-occupied Spain. He built a reputation as a captain who would not risk the safety of his crew unnecessarily, but was likely to make them rich with prize money.[5]

As previous generations of warfighters were well-aware, "safety" is about preserving combat strength and unit morale, not eliminating risk altogether.

The primary and alternate safety officers must complete the Collateral Duty Safety Officer Course within 30 days of their appointment.[6] Safety regulations contain numerous responsibilities, but at a minimum the following should be listed in their appointment counselings:

1. Work with the training room and platoon sergeants to ensure the unit complies with safety regulations. All soldiers must complete the online composite risk management training, have a valid Army Accident Avoidance certificate, and have their privately-owned vehicle inspected every 6 months.[7]

2. Integrate deliberate risk management into all missions/training activities[8] and forward the DD Form 2977 worksheets to the appropriate commander for approval.[9]

3. Coordinate with battalion and garrison safety officers for Standard Army Safety and Occupational Health Inspections (SASOHIs) for all work sites.[10]

---

[5] *The War for All the Oceans,* by Roy and Leslie Adkins
[6] AR 385-10 §10-8a, 27 November 2013
[7] AR 385-10 §9-3f, §11-7a and §11-8; 27 November 2013
[8] AR 385-10 §1-5c(7), 27 November 2013
[9] DA PAM 385-30 Table 4-1, 2 December 2014
[10] AR 385-10 §2-3d(2) and §17-6a, 27 November 2013

4. Investigate Class C through E accidents within the company and report the results through the Report It! website.[11]
5. Consolidate accident reports for the battalion's quarterly safety councils.[12]

Mandatory training requirements are best conducted prior to four-day weekends. If the training is online and produces a certificate, even better. Announce the requirement well before the long weekend, and require soldiers to turn in their certificate before they can be released. For most soldiers, an extra hour on the weekend is worth two during the work week.

Commissioned officers can serve as safety officers, but there are two restrictions that make them poor choices. First, safety officers must have at least 12 months remaining in the unit at the time of appointment.[13] Second, accident investigators are not permitted to share information with AR 15-6 investigating officers.[14] You don't want to use up a lieutenant on a safety investigation when you could use them for a 15-6.

In addition to the safety officers, the unit must have a primary and alternate radiation safety officer to manage the inventory of radioactive commodities in the unit.[15] In units that possess limited types of equipment, TRADOC-provided training is adequate, making the unit's 74D CBRN Specialist an ideal candidate.[16] For the alternate, select an NCO or officer who has supervisory authority over them and require them to complete the online radiation safety officer's course.

---

[11] AR 385-10 §3-15c, 27 November 2013. https://reportit.safety.army.mil/
[12] AR 385-10 §15-4, 27 November 2013
[13] AR 385-10 §2-6g(5), 27 November 2013
[14] AR 385-10 §3-10d(2), 27 November 2013
[15] DA PAM 385-24 §1-4r(4), 24 August 2007
[16] DA PAM 385-24 §7-2f, 24 August 2007

The Army publishes preliminary loss reports for every Class A accident, some of which offer useful lessons to present in safety briefs. You can sign up to receive these automatically via the ReportIt safety website.[17]

Safety Briefs

The weekly safety brief was never meant to be a mind-numbing speech given to soldiers before releasing them—it is supposed to inspire soldiers and remind them to do something constructive with their free time. In fact, when done correctly, safety briefs can be the most direct way to positively influence your unit.

Whatever you do, don't ever simply rattle off a list of "don'ts."—don't get drunk, don't abuse your spouse, don't get arrested, etc. Rather, dialogue with your soldiers about life, personal responsibility, and the promising futures that they and their loved ones have.[18] You don't have to be eloquent, but be sincere.

As a company commander, I spoke about my cousin who'd committed suicide, my father-in-law who'd grown up during the Korean War (in Korea), and a soldier from a former unit who'd died in a motorcycle accident. I did AARs of preliminary loss reports, gave examples of sports "character plays," and read the UCMJ actions taken against senior leaders. I wasn't always as succinct as they'd have liked, but I felt my soldiers deserved a well thought-out discourse on something real, and I believe they appreciated that.[19]

---

[17] https://reportit.safety.army.mil/
[18] *Taking the Guidon*, Nate Allen & Tony Burgess, 2001, p102.
[19] For more about being real with your people, see *Discovering your Authentic Leadership* from the February 2007 Harvard Business Review

Example Safety Brief Before releasing you for the weekend, I want to talk to you about character. In sports, a character play is one where a player is so focused on doing their job that they'll sacrifice themselves to make the play. Arguably the best character play in baseball was a double play by a Blue Jays catcher named Buck Martinez.

In baseball, a throw to home plate is always a tense situation. The catcher will try to catch the ball and tag a runner out, while the runner will run into the catcher as hard as he can to knock the ball out and score. In this situation, there was a runner on second base—a former Big Eight college football player named Phil Bradley. The batter, Gorman Thomas, hit what would normally be an RBI single to right field, but the right fielder charged the ball and threw to home plate to catch Bradley, who had rounded third.

Martinez, covering home plate, caught the ball in time to absorb the full impact of Bradley's charge. In the process, he suffered a broken leg and a severely dislocated ankle, but maintained control of the ball for the out. By this point, however, Thomas had reached second base and tried to reach third.

Martinez threw to third, but—injured and on the ground—missed the mark, sending the ball into left field. Seeing the errant throw, Thomas also decided to try for home plate, so the left fielder threw to Martinez for a second play at the plate. Despite the pain and being hobbled by his broken leg, Martinez caught the ball in time to lean back and tag Thomas for the second out. Martinez left the game on a stretcher, his only satisfaction that he had completed perhaps the only 9-2-7-2 double play in baseball history.

This weekend, I'm not asking you be some kind of hero. I don't want you to do things that might result in some kind of career-ending injury. But if you have the opportunity to stand up for what is right—to tell a battle buddy it's time to stop, or prevent some SHARP incident—I hope that you too will be willing to sacrifice what's comfortable, and make that 'character play' yourself. Dismissed.

---

[20] http://espn.go.com/blog/sweetspot/post/_/id/28631/the-greatest-play-ever-made; https://www.youtube.com/watch?v=kjHo1w_9WwM

Provide Command Emphasis

Safety briefs should not be the only times you discuss standards for right behavior. Show proper command emphasis for your Equal Opportunity (EO), Suicide Prevention, and Sexual Harassment/Assault Response Program (SHARP) by introducing the subject and the speaker for each brief.

"We always have time for the things we put first."—Steven Covey

Spend a few moments explaining *why* the program is important, and then provide a conclusion at the end. What you do with your time shows what's important to you; you show your priorities by taking the time to personally attend these briefs.

Equal Opportunity

Behaviors that undermine dignity and respect are fundamentally in opposition to the Army Values and are prohibited.[21] The goal of the equal opportunity program is to foster a workplace environment that is free from offensive behavior, where soldiers can thrive regardless of their background.

Appoint a SGT(P) or above as the Equal Opportunity Representative (EOR). If you haven't already drawn up the required command policy statements, have the EOR draft both the core policy and a second detailing complaint procedures.[22]

To gauge the baseline command climate, conduct a unit survey within your first 30 days. In the survey, you'll have the opportunity to select several short answer questions, so work with the first sergeant and the EOR to select a topic you want to learn more about. Choose the survey method you want to do the survey (online, small group discussion, etc).

[21] AR 600-20 §4-19, 6 November 2014
[22] AR 600-20 §6-3i(11), 6 November 2014

Once the results have been posted, provide feedback to the unit, stating what issues you see in the company and how you'll address them. Repeat the survey after six months to see if there is any improvement.[23]

There is an indisputable link between how soldiers are treated and how they perform their duties.[24] In addition to the EO policies, a separate policy about the prevention of hazing and bullying is needed.[25] Emphasize that any conduct deemed humiliating, harmful, or demeaning—whether in person or electronically—is in direct violation to regulations and is contrary to the kind of unit you are trying to build. Describe complaint procedures and explain that all complainants will be protected from reprisal.[26]

EO Complaints

Equal opportunity complaints can be registered either formally or informally. Informal complaints may be resolved directly by the individual or with the help of another person and do not need to be in writing. However, anyone working on the resolution of an informal complaint should prepare a memorandum of record detailing the actions taken.[27]

Formal complaints require the complainant to complete a DA Form 7279 Equal Opportunity Complaint Form, and to state the EO basis for the complaint (e.g. race, gender, national origin). Soldiers have 60 days from the date of the incident to file a formal complaint.[28]

As a commander, if you receive a formal complaint it behooves you to notify your battalion commander immediately. Formal complaints must be reported to the first General Courts-Martial Convening Authority (GCMCA) in the chain of command within three calendar days[29].

---

[23] AR 600-20 §6-3i(13), 6 November 2014
[24] AR 600-20 §5-13a, 6 November 2014
[25] AR 600-20 §4-19c(2), 6 November 2014
[26] AR 600-20 §4-19a, 6 November 2014
[27] AR 600-20 C-1a(1), 6 November 2014
[28] AR 600-20 C-1b, 6 November 2014
[29] AR 600-20 C-4a, 6 November 2014

After receipt of the complaint, commanders have 14 days to investigate the matter and provide written feedback to the complainants. If an extension is granted to the investigating officer, complainants are entitled to updates every 14 days until final resolution.[30] Derogatory information must be reported the security manager.[31]

> Headquarters and headquarters companies pose a special problems for company commanders, as they are responsible for the company's command climate but have limited authority over the staff. In this situation, the company commander can act as an ombudsman—someone who can advocate for complainants but are outside staff members' chain of command. Make sure to 'advertise' this role, as it will help the battalion commander identify problems before the command climate becomes toxic.

Prevention of Sexual Harassment

Sexual harassment is a form of gender discrimination that involves unwelcome sexual advances, requests for sexual favors, and other verbal or physical conduct of a sexual nature.[32] Your commitment to the dignity and respect of every soldier requires an uncompromising attitude on sexual harassment.

Commanders must publish and post a written command policy statement for the prevention of sexual harassment. It must state how and where to file complaints and that all complainants will be protected from acts or threats of reprisal.[33]

---

[30] AR 600-20 C-5 and C-7b(1), 6 November 2014
[31] AR 600-20 §4-19c(4), 6 November 2014
[32] AR 600-20 §7-4, 6 November 2014
[33] AR 600-20 §7-2b, 6 November 2014

One day, on a barracks inspection with a representative from the housing office, I saw that a soldier had posted some inappropriate pictures on the wall in their room—a violation of the sexual harassment policy against creating a hostile environment. To correct the problem, I spoke to the first sergeant and the soldier's section NCOIC.

To prevent a future one, I called a formation and offered a deal: no offensive pictures on walls, and I'd provide a binder to every person who wants one. (I even held up an example, complete with plastic covers to keep 'documents' from being soiled.) That way, no one would have to see them involuntarily, yet a person soldier could still offer to show the binder to any room guests. Anyone interested could see me after the formation.

A few giggled in the formation, but the outright laughter came afterward. Among those laughing in the back was the battalion commander, unseen until then, who'd arrived just in time to hear the speech.

No one asked for the binder, but everyone understood the standard.

Despite its association with sexual assault in the SHARP, sexual harassment complaints are handled in the same way as EO complaints—either formally or informally. To properly address an issue, commanders must be familiar with the categories of sexual harassment and how this kind of unacceptable behavior differs from sexual assault.

Sexual harassment may be verbal, nonverbal, or physical, and can take multiple forms. Verbal sexual harassment includes sexual jokes and inappropriate terms of endearment. Nonverbal sexual harassment includes sexual gestures and posting sexually oriented printed material. Physical contact includes unsolicited back or neck rubs.[34] Sexual harassment may also take the form of a *quid pro quo* as a condition for career opportunities.[35]

[34] AR 600-20 §7-5, 6 November 2014
[35] AR 600-20 §7-6, 6November 2014

Informal sexual harassment complaints might be best handled the unit level. Formal ones will require the battalion commander's immediate attention. A report of sexual assault, however, will involve a number of other parties.

Prevention of Sexual Assault

Sexual assault is a criminal offense that has no place in the Army.[36] Your position on sexual assault should be as clear in your conduct as it is in your policy statement and the literature posted around your unit area.[37]

A soldier, family member, or civilian who has been sexually assaulted has two reporting options: restricted and unrestricted. As the company commander, you will have no knowledge of restricted reports, as they can only be given confidentially to a health care provider, chaplain, sexual assault response coordinator (SARC), or unit victim advocate.[38]

If, however, you hear of a sexual assault, you have no choice but to report the incident through unrestricted channels.[39] A multitude of additional provisions apply to sexual assault cases—more than can be reviewed here—but the most important thing you can do is balance your responsibility to ensure community safety and the process of law with the duty to protect the victim's privacy and their need for dignity and respect.[40] Avoid re-victimizing the person with any questions about the experience, and report the matter to a SARC or victim advocate as soon as possible.

After the victim has been escorted to a SARC, contact the battalion commander, the Criminal Investigations Division (CID), and the staff judge advocate within 24 hours. Victims should also be encouraged to get a medical examination no matter when the incident occurred.[41]

[36] AR 600-20 §8-2a, 6 November 2014
[37] AR 600-20 §8-50(17), 6 November 2014
[38] AR 600-20 G-4a, 6 November 2014
[39] AR 600-20 G-5e, 6 November 2014
[40] AR 600-20 G-3, , 6 November 2014
[41] AR 600-20 §8-50(5)-(8), 6 November 2014, and AR 195-1

Suicide Prevention

Suicide prevention, as a program, requires proactive, caring, and coura-geous soldiers and civilians who can recognize danger and take imme-diate action to save a life.[42] The staff proponent for suicide prevention is typically the chaplain, because their training includes recognition of potential danger and warning signs, suicidal risk estimation, confiden-tiality requirements, how to conduct suicide prevention training, and intervention techniques.[43]

However, it will be almost impossible for either you—much less the chaplain—to keep tabs on the mental and behavioral health of every soldier. Successful suicide prevention will require you to train and enroll NCOs and junior enlisted soldiers to engage all ranks and demographics. Ask-Care-Escort—Suicide Intervention (ACE-SI) is a 4-hour module and one-time training requirement for all levels of company leadership, from your command team down to the squad leader. An additional 6-hour train-the-trainer module is also available.[44]

To arrange for intervention training, work with the S3 schools NCO or the contact the chaplain directly. Because depression is most prevalent during the holiday season, the best time to build a coterie of trained individuals is in the fall. Work with the first sergeant to identify members of the unit who will be most effective, and brief them before the course what your expectations are. There is also annual suicide prevention and awareness training that is required of all soldiers and Army civilians.[45]

Although suicide prevention is indeed a program to be monitored, treating it exclusively as "another Army program" would be a mistake. You can distribute risk reduction worksheets to everyone and enter the results into the Commander's Risk Reduction Database, but risk

[42] AR 600-63 §4-4, 14 April 2015
[43] AR 600-63 §4-5a(1) 14 April 2015 (d),
[44] AR 600-63 §4-7h, 14 April 2015
[45] AR 600-63 §4-7a, 14 April 2015. Found at http://www.preventsuicide.army.mil

identification still essentially relies on soldiers' self-reporting. Fulfill the requirements of the program, but minimize the bureaucracy that treats people as mere statistics.

PFC Brian Hutson committed suicide in Iraq by putting his M-4 rifle into his mouth and firing a three-round burst. He had done so after only a few months in the Army and even less time at the forward operating base he was assigned to. Nobody had really befriended him, though in a combat zone it is often hard to identify the new people you need to in order to prevent such losses.

At the required memorial service,[46] a young captain rose and spoke without notes, "I was his team leader but I never really knew him. Brian was new here. He didn't have no nickname and he didn't spend much time with us. He played Xbox a lot. We don't know why he committed suicide. We miss him anyway because he was one of us. That's all I have to say."[47]

You will not be able to personally give everyone the attention they deserve, but someone can. The loss of any individual, no matter how isolated, affects the whole unit—because they are one of you.

The human side of suicide prevention—the truly effective part—comes from a belief and perspective that at-risk soldiers are not a burden, and is a key element of your command climate. Never ostracize an at-risk soldier, and certainly not through special marking or clothing (such as a reflective vest).[48] Rather, recognize they are an integral part of the unit, members of the family. As such they deserve to be engaged, not shunned or humiliated. If you can de-stigmatize the positive act of seeking help, you can identify high-risk individuals early and possibly save a life.

---

[46] AR 600-20 §5-14a, 6 November 2014
[47] *We Meant Well*, Peter Van Buren, Metropolitan Books.
[48] AR 600-63 §1-31h, 14 April 2015

A Death in the Unit

If your unit loses a soldier—whether from suicide, accident, or other cause—a number of garrison and higher echelon parties will be involved to reduce the burden on your unit. Nevertheless, it's better to be prepared for such a possibility, so ask the chaplain for a copy of the garrison's notification and action flowchart.

If your battalion commander is not already aware, your first duty will be to contact them immediately. You will need to provide the Casualty Assistance Center with several documents, plus a DA Form 7747 if suicide is suspected.[49] Depending on circumstances, a Casualty Notification Officer will be appointed to contact the next of kin. Afterward, a pre-designated Casualty Assistance Officer will begin assisting the family with funeral preparation and other financial matters.[50]

Next, brief the unit on what occurred within 24 hours. The purpose will be to control the inevitable rumors that will circulate, preclude speculation about the cause of death, and prevent soldiers from putting confidential information on social media. They should know that an AR 15-6 investigation will look into events, and that they should keep any comments for sworn statements.[51]

A summary court martial officer will be appointed to recover any Army property and inventory personal effects for the next of kin; your supply sergeant or barracks manager should assist with the inventory.[52] Finally, you should prepare some comments about the deceased. You will probably have a speaking role at the memorial that will take place.[53]

---

[49] DA PAM 638-8 Table 4-1, 23 June 2015, and AR 600-63 §1-31w, 14 April 2015
[50] AR 638-8 §5-2a(1), , 23 June 2015
[51] AR 600-63 §1-31s, 14 April 2015
[52] AR 638-2 §18-1, 22 December 2000
[53] AR 600-20 §5-14a, 6 November 2014

Army Substance Abuse Program (ASAP)

The first goal of the ASAP is to deter substance abuse; the second is to identify and then rehabilitate substance abusers.[54] To set up the program, you first need two E5s or higher to serve as primary and alternate Unit Prevention Leaders (UPLs).[55] The two UPLs will need appointment letters and certification, which can be arranged through the S3's schools NCO. Require that they produce a unit substance abuse SOP for your signature within 30 days after they receive certification.[56]

In addition, you will need a cadre of male and female personnel, E-5 or higher, to serve as observers.[57] The observers may rotate, but must be briefed on their duties and sign a Urinalysis Observation Briefing Memorandum before performing their duties.[58] Work with the first sergeant to select qualified personnel, then counsel them on their responsibilities.

> *"Officers who fail to perform their duty in correcting small violations and in enforcing proper conduct are in capable of leading."*
> —*General George S. Patton, Jr. April 1943*

As commander, you choose the day and time for the tests. The primary UPL will select personnel on a random basis for testing. Once notified, soldiers have no more than two hours to report.[59] Although this is usually done during PT hours to avoid impacting the training schedule, it is important to be unpredictable. Test at the end of the duty day, during field exercises, or on back-to-back days. Work with the UPL to determine the dates and times.

---

[54] AR 600-85 B-1, 28 December 2012
[55] AR 600-85 B-3a, 28 December 2012
[56] AR 600-85 §2-33n, 28 December 2012
[57] AR 600-85 §4-9c(1), 28 December 2012
[58] AR 600-85 §4-9d, 28 December 2012; see Figure E-4 for an example
[59] AR 600-85 §4-3c(2), 28 December 2012

During the test, you'll read the commander's urinalysis briefing, and the UPL will read the unit brief.[60] After all samples are collected, the UPL will submit the product for testing and should provide you with a back-brief on the results.

In the past, units were responsible for performing a 4 percent weekly urinalysis, which proved burdensome. Because of absences due to missions, leave, TDY, and schools, units often had to select 10 percent of personnel to get the 4 percent. This changed in 2016 to a monthly 10 percent requirement across each battalion.[61] While the change in policy reduces the burden on individual companies, it requires greater coordination with the battalion-level UPL.

Once urinalysis procedures are set, shift your focus to identification and rehabilitation. If you have a positive urinalysis result refer to AR 600-85 Table B-2 for the outline of the process. Assuming you have illegal drug use, you'll have to contact law enforcement, flag the soldier, and possibly begin a commander's inquiry. The soldier will also require a referral to ASAP within five duty days.[62] A second incident of misconduct within 12 months requires you to initiate separation proceedings.[63]

Although illegal drug use is a problem, a more common issue is alcohol abuse and underage drinking. These situations, too, require a referral the soldiers for ASAP counseling within five working days using DA Form 8003.[64] Of course, this is in addition to whatever UCMJ action you decide on.

The appendices to AR 600-85 provide superb guides for a good urinalysis program. Appendix B is the guide for commanders. Appendix D provides an assessment checklist. Guidance for the SOP is in Appendix E. Review these documents with the UPLs after your first three months.

---

[60] AR 600-85 E-2 and E-3, 28 December 2012
[61] Army Directive 2016-15, 22 April 2016
[62] AR 600-85 §2-33m, 28 December 2012
[63] AR 600-85 §1-7c(5), 28 December 2012
[64] AR 600-85 §3-2c, 28 December 2012

One way to find out what's going on is to eat at the DFAC on non-payday weekends. Wear civilian clothes so your soldiers know you're not there in an 'official' capacity. Invite soldiers to sit with you. Listen and watch the non-verbal communication. This will tell you more than any command climate survey.

Comprehensive Soldier & Family Fitness (CSF2)

While the previously listed programs aim to prevent and mitigate negative issues, CSF2 is more concerned about promoting positive habits and overall wellness. Its goal is to reduce potential problems by improving the physical and psychological health and resilience of soldiers and their families.[65] This makes it a particularly good program to offer to the Family Readiness Group (FRG).

Ideally, each company has at least one Master Resiliency Trainer (ASI 8R)[66] who serves as your advisor[67] and trains the company in all 12-24 resilience skills at least once a year.[68] Additionally, the MRT should incorporate informal resilience training into daily activities, training, and operational events. To prevent the training schedule from becoming too packed, one best practice is to combine resiliency training with physical training, FRG meetings, or a Friday formation.[69]

Unfortunately, two things will prevent you from completely reaching the CSF2 program's stated goals—time and training money. (On top of all the mandated company level training, each soldier is supposed to receive training in all five performance enhancement areas—a task that has been difficult to implement from the program's outset.[70]) The CSF2 program was promoted as a way to reduce the suicide rate, but

---

[65] Army Directive 2013-07, 25 March 2013, as found on the Ready and Resilient website
[66] AR 350-1 G-24e(1), 19 August 2014
[67] Army Directive 2013-07, Enclosure 2 §2a
[68] Army Directive 2013-07, Enclosure 4 §2 lists 12, though the program offers 24
[69] Army Directive 2013-07, Enclosure 4 §3
[70] Army Directive 2013-07, Enclosure 4 §7

the program has relied on individual units to collect and input completion rates for each task.[71] As you can guess, it has been difficult to prove extent of the CSF2 program's effectiveness,[72] and it has since become a "back-burner" issue for many commanders.

> *"You cannot expect a soldier to be a proud soldier if you humiliate him. You cannot expect him to be brave if you abuse and cower him. You cannot expect him to fight and die for our cause if your soldier has not been treated with the respect and dignity which fosters unit esprit and personal pride."—GEN Delos Emmons*

Nevertheless, each soldier is required to complete the Global Assessment Tool (GAT) annually as a way to gauge their mental and behavioral health.[73] (To find out who has completed theirs, you can request "Leader Access" once you've completed the GAT yourself.) Once a soldier does this, they will be able to access the ArmyFit website, where they can find a number of resources to help them reach personal goals. Family members who are registered in DEERS are able to access these as well.

While competing requirements keep the CSF2 program from achieving its full potential, it is perhaps most beneficial for your medium-risk soldiers and families—those who are going through difficulties, but aren't experiencing a crisis. If you can at least identify and help this group on a regular basis through the CSF2 program, you've done what you can to fulfill its intent.

Promoting Health

Beyond the formal programs, you have a continuing responsibility to encourage "a lifestyle that improves and protects physical, behavioral, and spiritual well-being: including maintaining a tobacco-free lifestyle, a healthy body-mass composition, and adequate sleep."[74]

[71] ALARACT 128/2013 §1 and 2D
[72] Comprehensive Soldier & Family Fitness website, Technical Report #4
[73] AR 350-1 G-24g(2), 19 August 2014
[74] AR 600-63 §1-31a, 14 April 2015

Some things are fairly straightforward. Enforce mouth guard use during combatives and on confidence courses.[75] Nutritional fitness is a good thing.[76] Proper furniture and office hardware make for good ergonomics.[77] However, once you start enforcing the policy on tobacco use, you might get some pushback.

> If you want a reputation as an Army professional who knows and follows the rules, put AR 600-63 §7-3a into effect. Some Army leaders dismiss this regulation; many more remain unfamiliar with it. Meanwhile, knowledgeable NCOs and soldiers quietly scorn their ignorance.

The Army's official policy on tobacco in the workplace is surprisingly strict: "Tobacco use is prohibited in all DA-occupied workplaces except for designated smoking areas."[78] This applies to both smoking and smokeless tobacco (dip), in offices and in field tents, whether on or off duty. Technically speaking, people who dip need to go outside to a designated smoking area, which is at least 50 feet away from a common point of entry.

This may seem extreme, but remember—you are the unit's conscience. You as the commander should set the highest standards of personal conduct. It's your job to make sure today's leaders set good examples so that junior soldiers can grow into tomorrow's role models for future soldiers.

Chaplains and Military Family Life Consultants

At times, soldiers will have issues for which there is no right or wrong answer. They will have family issues in distant parts of the United States, marriage issues they won't want to bring to their supervisor, and professional issues they'll want confidentiality to freely discuss. Your duty is to

---

[75] AR 600-63 §5-5b1(c), 14 April 2015
[76] AR 600-63 §5-6, 14 April 2015
[77] AR 600-63 §5-4, 14 April 2015
[78] AR 600-30 §7-3a, 14 April 2015

reduce the stigma associated with seeking help and refer individuals experiencing personal problems.[79]

Chaplains are good for this, and there is one for each battalion. Apart from life-threatening situations, they can maintain confidentiality and can provide a wide range of counseling options. (As discussed earlier, they can also provide training for suicide prevention.) Plus, as soldiers themselves, chaplains deploy with their headquarters units, providing continuity for the unit during its most stressful transitions.[80]

A second option is the Military Family Life Consultant (MFLC). These professional civilian counselors are assigned at the brigade level, and are ideal if someone prefers a counselor without religious affiliation. They too have strict confidentiality requirements—they will not discuss when or even if they have an appointment with someone. This confidentiality encourages soldiers to discuss their issues more openly, since they can be confident the chain of command will not be involved. And because MFLCs are civilian employees, family members often feel more comfortable with MFLCs than with chaplains.

Although confidentiality rules prevent the MFLC from informing you of any meetings with soldiers, referrals are still possible. One method is to invite the MFLC to your office (perhaps a little before lunch) and bring the soldier in. Explain that—based on what you've seen or heard the soldier is going through—you think they'd benefit from a talk with the MFLC. You explain the rules—that you will never know what they discuss or if they will ever meet again—and then come back after lunch (just ask the MFLC to lock the door when they leave).

In this way, you can know that the soldier at least spoke with a counselor, while also respecting the MFLC's confidentiality rules. Just be sure to communicate this with the MFLC when you schedule the appointment.

---

[79] AR 600-63 §1-31bb and ee, 14 April 2015
[80] AR 600-63 §4-3d(1), 14 April 2015

Family Readiness Group

The Family Readiness Group (FRG) is a semi-official group comprised of family members who are organized for mutual support. As the new commander, building a successful FRG is tricky business, but the first step is contacting Army Community Services (ACS).

ACS provides training assistance for both new commanders and FRG leaders[81]. In particular, it can explain the different roles required by a successful FRG (treasurer, key caller, welcome committee chair) to both you and the volunteers who will fill those roles. This is important because FRG volunteers are to be supervised in the same manner as employees, and may be allocated office space and computers in government facilities to perform their duties. [82]

With the FRG's leadership established, look to ascertain what each family needs so that you can develop a feel for what direction the FRG should take. Generally speaking, people look to the FRG for information, assisted living, and/or social contacts.[83]

The ones who seek information want to know what the unit is doing and how the unit's schedule will affect home life. For them, a newsletter or periodic broadcast email is sufficient for their needs, but they may be open to greater involvement. To develop their interest in Army life further, refer this group to the Army Family Team Building (AFTB) program's Level I curriculum.[84]

The second group will have diverse needs, ranging from a newcomer asking advice about the area, to a spouse looking for a babysitter, or a family who has serious life management issues. For them, the FRG is an additional resource in the community.

---

[81] AR 608-1 §4-6, 13 March 2013
[82] AR 608-1 J-4a, 13 March 2013.
[83] *Muddy Boots Leadership*, by John Chapman. p75
[84] AR 608-1 M-3a, 13 March 2013

The third group—the spouses who are looking for social contacts — is often open to filling roles of responsibility for the group. For them, the FRG offers opportunities to meet new people, have a positive impact on families, and do something meaningful. For them, AFTB Level II and III will help develop their skills.

> *"Each of us is the company."—William Hewlitt*

If meeting with families individually is not possible, schedule time with the FRG leader individually or chair the first meeting yourself. To get maximum participation, have the first sergeant create a contact roster of all family members in the unit and invite each spouse personally. Do this far enough in advance that spouses have a reasonable amount of time to plan for it.

Meetings should discuss the training calendar in a meaningful way. Cover field, red cycle, and block leave times so that families can schedule events like vacations and birthday parties. If members are open to quarterly events, plan fundraisers (if necessary) and ask who is willing to be the project point of contact. This way, you know who's responsible, the FRG leader doesn't burn out, and you're maintaining the FRG's volunteer nature. It's better to have fewer, higher quality events than risk overloading the calendar.

Look to combine FRG events with hails and farewells in various locations outside the company area. The on-post bowling alley can be a fun location, especially when the bumpers are installed for the kids, and there is always the ACS center, which has the facilities for child care.

The purpose of a newsletter is to keep family members informed and to publicize accomplishments. It should report on the unit's training activities, spotlight soldiers' achievements, and list family members' special days (e.g. birthdays, anniversaries, etc.). When young, single soldiers are spotlighted, have a copy of the newsletter sent to their parents, along with a photo from the event.

As new families come into the unit, conduct house visits to understand what their needs are. Some specific questions to answer are:

- Where do they live—on-post or off, and which neighborhood?

- Is the spouse working or looking for a job?

- How are any children cared for? What's their day care situation?

- Is anyone sick in the family, or an Exceptional Family Member?

- Are the children school-age? How are the children adjusting to a new school?

- How has the work schedule been? Are unrealistic work schedules hurting family life?

- What are their expectations of the FRG?

For house visits, give families the courtesy of advance notice, and bring a small welcome gift. The purpose is to make families feel welcome, and establish a line of communication. Spouses will feel much more comfortable coming to meetings if they've met you beforehand.

You know you have a great FRG when members welcome incoming families and communicate needs among themselves. It's possible, but it requires a commitment at your level, a light touch, and a genuine concern for your soldiers and their families.

Family Advocacy Program

Moving from place to place places stress on families, and not everyone is in a position to successfully deal with that stress. The family with no car, little money, no extended family support, and four children is a potential powder keg of problems. The Family Readiness Group can take care of small, temporary issues, but FRG members are volunteers, and when families have trouble adjusting to Army life the FRG can only go so far.

If the military police are called for suspected child neglect or domestic abuse, the Family Advocacy Program (FAP) will be brought in. Their purpose is "to break the cycle of abuse by identifying abuse as early as possible and providing treatment for affected family members."[85]

FAP will look at home life and create a case file on the family. As the commander, your job will be to attend the Case Review Committee hosted by the garrison commander and offer your opinion on the case.[86] At a minimum, counseling and Good Parenting classes will be advised, and you should regularly report the family's situation in the battalion commander's Risk Reduction meetings. More serious cases will involve a wider array of authorities that will reduce your relative responsibility on the matter.

Family Care Plans

Some families are particularly sensitive to disruption. Dual-military parents, single parents, and those with certain custody agreements must make plans to ensure family members are "adequately cared for when the soldier is deployed, on TDY, or otherwise not available due to military requirements."[87] This means developing a Family Care Plan.

As the commander, you may delegate Family Care Plan counseling, but you are the sole approving authority for the DA Form 5305. Soldiers should have 30 days from the date of the counseling to complete their plan. If they cannot complete one within that time, you have the authority to initiate either a bar to continued service or involuntary separation procedures. [88]

---

[85] AR 608-38 §1-5c, 30 October 2007
[86] AR 608-38 §2-3b(5), 30 October 2007
[87] AR 600-20 §5-5b, 6 November 2014
[88] AR 600-20 §5-5g, 6 November 2014

Family Support

Commanders have the responsibility to ensure soldiers understand their obligations to provide family support on a continuing basis.[89] Nevertheless, you may receive a complaint from a separated spouse alleging non-support during your time in command. Your duty will be to investigate every inquiry alleging financial non-support and provide a complete and accurate report to the individual making the inquiry.[90]

Not every inquiry is a foregone conclusion, so make sure you appoint someone who will fairly and objectively investigate the matter. Separation agreements and custody issues quickly complicate matters, so be sure to work with the staff judge advocate in reaching a conclusion.

Better Opportunities for Single Soldiers (BOSS)

While the FRG primarily supports on married soldiers, the BOSS program focuses on fun events for singles. It may be organized by either the garrison or individual units.

If run by individual units, develop a BOSS council comprised of one representative per platoon and a company primary. The BOSS council should select a quarterly activity and bring it to you and the first sergeant for approval. The company primary can make the arrangements and publicize the event, then coordinate for resources (such as renting a bus).

If it is run by the garrison, select a primary and alternate BOSS representative and ensure they have the time to attend the garrison's BOSS meetings. Their job will be to provide visibility on all BOSS events and trips, so supply a cork board that they can post flyers onto. In addition, invite them to speak to the formation on Fridays so they can advertise upcoming events.

---

[89] AR 608-99 §5-2, 29 October 2003
[90] AR 608-99 §3-6, 29 October 2003

Warrior Adventure Quest (WAQ)

Another program to boost unit morale is the WAQ. It was originally designed "to introduce re-deploying soldiers with activities that serve as alternatives to aberrant behaviors," but is open to all units, and offer a fantastic opportunity for soldiers to have fun.[91] Events include rock climbing, mountain biking, ropes courses, skiing, and ziplining.

The first step to taking advantage of the program is to select at least two staff sergeants or above to serve as event leaders and attend the required training. After the activity is complete, the event leaders must administer a debriefing and submit completed surveys back to the WAQ office.

Volunteerism

Motivated soldiers who are interested in distinguishing themselves can be awarded the Military Outstanding Volunteer Service Medal (MOVSM) if they accrue enough volunteer hours.[92] Battalion commanders are the approving authority; just be sure to find out what the hours threshold is before you recommend someone.

To ensure volunteers are properly recognized and documented, appoint an NCO and have them contact Army Community Services to receive training on the Volunteer Management Information System (VMIS)[93]. If your unit participates in a Good Neighbor or Adopt-a-School Program, ask if these hours count.

Financial Management

First term soldiers are frequently vulnerable to exploitation by the many unscrupulous financing institutions found around military facilities. To help prevent soldiers from accumulating more debt than they can rea-

---

[91] http://www.armymwr.com/recleisure/waq.aspx
[92] AR 600-2-22 §2-23, 11 December 2006
[93] AR 608-1 C-3, 13 March 2013

sonably handle, Army Community Services (ACS) provides the required 8 hours of financial management readiness training they must receive within their first three months.[94]

Soldiers who have fallen victim to such practices can also receive support from ACS in filing a formal consumer complaint via DA Form 5184[95]. Such reports are collected and at the garrison level and will help in having the institution removed from the list of approved establishments.

Serious Incident Reports

The different echelons of your chain of command will have different standards for what constitutes a serious incident. By regulation, the Department of the Army collects reports on Category I and Category II events. As a result, these are the ones of greatest interest to general officers.

At the company level, Category I and II events are rare, though of course you can do your part by not losing any sensitive items.[96] Of more significance to you will be your battalion commander's guidance, which will be available through the S-3. You should also request an example report.[97]

> Depending on the command climate, higher echelon commanders may take a surprisingly intense interest in what steps you've taken to prevent serious incidents. Discuss with your battalion commander what they expect to see in the Remarks section of the serious incident report.

Keep templates of these files on your home computer, and install a Common Access Card (CAC) reader. That way, if you have a serious incident in your unit, you can log on to the enterprise webmail instead of going to the office to complete the paperwork. (Serious incidents have a tendency to happen when you're already at home.)

---

[94] AR 608-1 §4-38, 13 March 2013
[95] AR 608-1 §4-44, 13 March 2013
[96] AR 190-45 §8-3d and h, 30 March 2007
[97] If the S-3 doesn't have one, build one using AR 190-45 Figure 9-4 as a template.

Red Cross

The Red Cross provides a number of instruction courses that may be of interest to soldiers. They can train lifeguards in water safety, babysitters in child care and first aid, and home caretakers of the sick and injured.[98] Course schedules are good information to provide to the FRG.

More important for commanders are Red Cross messages. If a soldier's immediate family member becomes critically ill, the Red Cross provides third party messaging directly from doctors to help you make emergency leave decisions.[99]

Typically, Red Cross messages are communicated through the staff duty desk, and will include whether the affected soldier is already aware of the situation or not. Assuming they are, contact the first sergeant to help with emergency leave paperwork. Depending on the soldier's finances, an Army Emergency Relief (AER) loan may also be necessary.

Emergency leave is a no-brainer for immediate family members, but things become difficult if you have to establish the five-year *in loco parentis* relationship. To preclude any last minute problems, ask if there are any such relationships when soldiers in-process.

Situations involving family members that don't meet the criteria for emergency leave can still be approved for ordinary leave. This would include childbirth, passing of a grandparent, or severe marital problems.[100] Be very careful about flat-out disapproving a soldier's leave request in these circumstances.

---

[98] AR 930-5 §2-1g, 1 February 2005
[99] AR 930-5 §2-1c, 1 February 2005
[100] AR 600-8-10 §6-1, 15 February 2006

Risk Reduction

Higher echelon commanders will want to know who the at-risk soldiers are in your formation and what you are doing about it. And while it is often impossible to effectively *prevent* something bad from happening, your raters' perceptions of your performance will be based on the way you handle difficult situations.

Battalion commanders usually want weekly updates from their command and legal teams on the status of soldiers who are at-risk and/or facing legal actions. These Risk Reduction/Legal Review Meetings are usually hosted by the chaplain or legal representative.

You can determine who in the company is at-risk by reviewing the complete list of risk factors found in AR 600-85 Table 12-1. Identify who is dealing with these kinds of issues with the first sergeant, and develop a plan of action for each person. Consult with the legal team about the feasibility of each person's plan of action before you brief the battalion commander in the risk reduction meeting.

In the past, the Army has had difficulty keeping visibility on at-risk soldiers as they transfer from unit to unit. Soldiers who went through ASAP counseling at one duty station wouldn't tell anyone in their new unit, and commanders wouldn't find out until another issue had surfaced.

To remedy this, the Army instituted the Commander's Risk Reduction Database (CRRD) as a way to track at-risk soldiers.[101] Company commanders request access through their battalion commanders, and can access the past two years of a soldier's risk events history. As new risk factors arise, you can update files so that no soldier is overlooked as they PCS to their next duty station.

---

[101] AR 600-85 §12-1, 28 December 2012

> *"There is no type of human endeavor where it is so important that the leader understands all phases of his job as that of the profession of arms."*—MG James C. Fry

Community Health Promotion Council (CHPC)

CHPC meetings are a way for the senior commander to receive feedback on garrison health and safety programs. Major tenant commanders, such as your brigade commander, are invited to discuss concerns that arise from within their organizations.[102]

Brigade commanders often use this opportunity not only to find out about current issues that face families, but also to evaluate their company commanders. Contact the person who compiles the slide deck and ask for a copy of the top performing commander's slides as a benchmark for your company's efforts.

Keeping the Best (Retention)

While every soldier's service is appreciated, only soldiers of high moral character, personal competence, and demonstrated adaptability to the requirements of the professional soldier's moral code may be reenlisted.[103] As the company's sole retention officer, you should evaluate all potential re-enlistees under this "whole person" concept.[104]

Your first step in developing the Retention Program is to appoint a Retention NCO. This person's responsibility will be to maintain records on each soldier and notify you when reenlistment interviews are coming up.[105] In coordination with the first sergeant, the retention NCO should draft a reenlistment incentive program for your approval (four day passes are typical).[106]

---

[102] AR 600-85 §12-1, 14 April 2015
[103] Army Directive 2016-19 Enclosure 1 §8-2a and AR 601-280 §8-2a, 31 January 2006
[104] AR 601-280 §2-2e and §3-7a, 31 January 2006
[105] AR 601-280 §2-2i(3), 31 January 2006
[106] AR 601-280 §1-5c(2), 31 January 2006

In the second month of a soldier's arrival at the unit, have the soldier speak with the battalion career counselor about their short and long term goals, career expectations, and steps to accomplish those goals. In the third month, you should follow up with the soldier to inform them of negative and positive aspect of current performance, as well as methods to overcome shortcomings. If the soldier shows limited future potential or difficulty in adapting to the Army, this is the time to consider instituting a Bar to Continued Service, as it will allow maximum time for rehabilitation.[107]

Talk to soldiers again when they reach about 15 to 16 months before their ETS date. For quality soldiers who are undecided, take the time to help them analyze their abilities, opportunities, limitations, and personal problems. If they have firmly decided to leave active service, support their decision, but recommend the Reserve Components. Those who will attend university should be informed of the Simultaneous Membership Program.

The Soldier For Life—Transition Assistance Program (the successor to ACAP) begins roughly one year from a soldier's termination of service. Soldiers need this time to properly plan for civilian life—those who are unprepared are at a severe disadvantage

Check in with the retention NCO on at least a monthly basis to see which interviews are coming up. To make things less formal, visit soldiers where they work rather than calling them to see you (no one likes getting called to the commander's office).

When soldiers reenlist, make sure the event is first class. Position a photographer, plan opening remarks, and recognize guests. Memorize the oath of enlistment—do not read it off an index card. After administering the oath, present the spouse with a certificate of appreciation, and close with the soldier's remarks.[108]

---

107 AR 601-280 Table C-1, 31 January 2006
108 AR 601-280 D-4, 31 January 2006

Bars to Continued Service

Soldiers who do not meet the aforementioned standards for reenlistment deserve to be notified so that they can overcome their deficiencies. The purpose of a bar to continued service is to formally notify poor performers and set standards for rehabilitation. If they cannot correct their deficiencies, they may be separated.

Untrainable or unsuitable soldiers, two-time APFT failures, those who cannot complete a mandatory Family Care Plan, and those who consistently fail to abide by military expectations are the primary candidates for bars. For instance, a specialist who meets minimum standards for their current rank but lacks the potential to be an NCO may be deemed untrainable and considered for a bar.[109]

With the concurrence of the first sergeant and the first line supervisor, a company commander's first step in barring a soldier will be to confer with the battalion commander as the approving authority. Once you've "pre-cleared" the bar, work with the career counselor or retention NCO to draw up the DA Form 4126.

Take, for example, a soldier who consistently fails to qualify on their assigned weapon, despite remedial training. Bring the soldier in, counsel them on their deficiency, and inform them that they will be flagged until they can qualify. The soldier will have an opportunity to provide a statement within seven days, after which time the career counselor will submit the 4126 to the command sergeant major for the battalion commander's signature. With the approval authority's signature, the soldier must be counseled again that the bar has been approved and that they will have their first review in 90 days.[110]

If that soldier is able to qualify on their weapon within 90 days, submit a recommendation to lift the bar to the battalion commander. If approved, counsel the soldier that the bar has been lifted, and lift the flag as well. If,

[109] Army Directive 2016-19 Enclosure 1, §8-4, 26 May 2016
[110] Army Directive 2016-19 Enclosure 1, K-4, 26 May 2016

however, 90 days have passed and that soldier is still not able to qualify, conduct the first review (again, with the first sergeant and career counselor present). Again, if that soldier is able to qualify in the next three months, great. Yet if the deficiency remains after six months, it's time to begin separation proceedings.[111]

Bars to continued service are great tools, but you must remember that they are rehabilitative in nature, not a back door method to separate troublemakers. Bar initiations must set concrete goals for soldiers, and once they reach those goals, they should at least be recognized for overcoming a personal challenge.

Health of the Force

Company commanders have two ways to track soldiers' physical profiles: eProfile and MEDPROS. To view soldier's DA Form 3349 profiles, check eProfile at least once a week, and download the PDF files for quick reference. Use MEDPROS to get a summary of the unit's profiles—both temporary and permanent—and to identify those who came into the unit with profiles.

> It is a common misperception that company commanders can override soldiers' profiles, and that profiles are not valid until the company commander signs them. In fact, the approval authorities for profiles are set by the Military Treatment Facility commander.[112] Any commander who believes they have the competency and authority to countermand a physician's instructions is not only risking their soldier's long-term health but their own career.

MEDPROS also tracks the length of each profile, which is useful for profile review meetings. Many units meet regularly with physicians to review soldiers' temporary profiles and see which ones look like a permanent condition. In these situations, a soldier might be evaluated for a perma-

[111] AR 635-200 §1-47, 6 June 2005
[112] AR 40-501 §7-11a(3)(j), 14 December 2007

nent level 3 ("P3") profile, which would require them to be evaluated by a Medical Evaluation Board and considered for separation.[113]

SIGACTS/Storyboards

Companies have two methods to trumpet their weekly accomplishments: Significant Actions (SIGACTS) and Storyboards. The SIGACTS are usually typewritten documents that describe what the unit trained on, list personal accomplishments, and address how the company fits into the brigade's lines of effort. Storyboards do the same thing, but graphically.

> *"If anything goes bad, then I did it. If anything goes semi-good, then we did it. If anything goes real good, then you did it."—Paul Bear Bryant*

As the company commander, you'll want to appoint a company public affairs officer and plan these out. Consider unit training events, ranges, reenlistments, volunteer activities, WAQ events, staff rides, and any other action that fits into the brigade's priorities. The goal is to show the battalion and brigade commanders how you're making them look good. Contact the S-3 for examples you can benchmark.

---

[113] AR 40-501 §7-4b(1), 14 December 2007

Storyboard Example

HHC, 498th CSSB
LOE: Strengthening the Alliance

Who: HHC, 498th CSSB
What: Nakdong Battle Reeanctment
Where: Daegu
When: 25 SEP 14
Summary: CW2 ▮▮▮▮ and SFC ▮▮▮▮ took 40 employees of the SP60 Supply and Services Facility to the Nakdong reenactment to celebrate the U.S. – South Korean alliance.

Employees of Camp Carroll's SP60 enjoy the Nakdong Battle Reenactment on Thursday, September 25th.

Champions!

Officer Professional Development

The Army has three ways to train leaders: institutional training, operational job experience, and self-development.[114] When lieutenants arrive at your unit, they will have completed their Basic Officer Leader Course institutional training. Your job will be to invest in their professional development so that one day they, too, can be successful company commanders.

Difference accession experiences produce lieutenants with different skill sets. Military academies generally produce highly skilled graduates who have matured as adults being surrounded by military culture, but are used to dealing with peers rather than enlisted personnel.

> *"Don't begrudge the time you spend developing, coaching, and helping your people to grow so they can carry on when you're gone. It's one of the best signs of good leadership".—Bernard Baruch*[115]

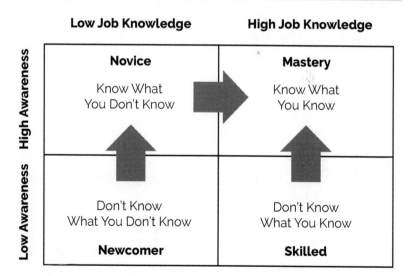

---

[114] AR 350-1 §1-11, 19 August 2014
[115] DA PAM 600-65, 1 November 1985

Lieutenants with prior service often make excellent company grade officers because of what they learned in their enlisted years. They also have a good understanding of how the Army *really* works—what's really important and what's not. Despite this, their timelines can sometimes weaken their potential in their field-grade years, and they're sometimes less open to learning new ideas from a less experienced captain.

Reserve Officer Training Corps (ROTC) lieutenants without any prior service tend to vary in quality depending on their school programs, but can show a lot of potential if mentored well. Similarly, enlistment-option officer candidate school graduates possess a wide range of skill sets, though they may require help in understanding their roles in the military world.

Depending on the job knowledge and personal awareness they've gained up to the time they join your unit, lieutenants fall into one of four developmental types: Newcomer, Novice, Skilled, and Mastery.

The majority of lieutenants start off as Newcomers. They may feel confident, but they simply don't know how much they don't know. They may be great at writing operations orders, but that's not a necessary skill as a platoon leader. To get the most out of this group, you need to explain what exactly what they need to learn in order to be effective.

Within a few weeks, reality will have set in and the Newcomer realizes just how little they know. At this point, they are a Novice—self-aware but still with little job knowledge. The goal for the Novice is to acquire the requisite skill set to be successful as a platoon leader, and then as an executive officer.

Lieutenants with prior enlisted service take a different route. They know what needs to be done, even if they can't always teach it or supervise others. This group comes in Skilled, just not fully mature. The goal for these lieutenants is to detach themselves from performing tasks they knew how to do quite well, and focus more on supervision and mentorship.

The goal is for each lieutenant to achieve Mastery of platoon leadership, and then to repeat the process as the Executive Officer or Operations Officer. As you meet your lieutenants, try to gauge where they're at and what they still need to learn. By the time they are promoted to first lieutenant, a platoon leader should at least have a Novice's knowledge of how to be an Executive Officer.

Now, asking a company commander to invest time in their lieutenants may sound daunting, but building strong lieutenants allows you to expand your influence over your company. When lieutenants understand the "big picture" of what your goals are, they'll be able to address your concerns before you even voice them.

> *"Use your people by allowing everyone to do his job. When a subordinate is free to do his job, he perceives this trust and confidence from his superiors and takes more pride in his job, himself, and the organization's goals and objectives. Delegation of sufficient authority and proper use of subordinates helps develop future leaders. This is a moral responsibility of every commander."—LTC Stanley Bonta*

If you refuse to take an active role in developing lieutenants, you won't get the most out of them. If they lack visibility on problems, they'll be little more than a figureheads. If you don't assign responsibility, they'll be little more than a consultant for the platoon sergeant—perhaps useful only for their computer skills. And if they don't understand how to use authority, they'll end up micromanaging their sergeants.

Rather, you want people who are platoon LEADERS. This mean giving them visibility, assigning responsibility, granting authority, and holding them accountable. But first, you must build their capabilities by integrating them into company operations.

When an NCO tells an officer, "This is NCO business," what are they really saying?

Depending on the context, it can mean either "I'll take care of it for you," or "Leave me alone." The former is a recognition that commissioned officers should focus on systems rather than individual soldier deficiencies. The latter is a rejection of the officer's authority and comes from either lack of experience, fear of incompetence, lack of confidence, or they're hiding something.

When an officer tells an NCO, "That's NCO business," it means "I don't care," and is an equally unacceptable rejection of responsibility. There's only one kind of business in the Army—leader business. NCOs advise, and officers decide. The scope of one's focus may be different, but the goal is the same: to build an excellent organization.

The majority of a new lieutenant's first thirty days is spent in-processing. In your first conversation with them, assign the following tasks:

- Complete all battalion and company in-processing, including mandatory online training (S-6 certificates, Anti-Terrorism Level 1, Accident Avoidance, Deliberate Risk Management, Commander's Safety Course, etc). Submit their certificates and APFT scorecard to the training room.

- Complete a one page biographical sketch to bring to an office call with the battalion commander (since their Officer Record Brief will be sparse)

- Schedule a date to draw TA-50

- Read the command philosophy, plus battalion and company policy letters

- Talk with the first sergeant about the role of the NCO

- Schedule a date for Driver's Training. Even if the lieutenant will never drive a vehicle, they need to know how to do and supervise PMCS.

- Review your OER support form and the battalion commander's

- Complete a draft initial counseling for their platoon sergeant/NCO

Next, introduce the lieutenant's sponsor and arrange for the following:

- An introduction to the platoon sergeant/NCO

- A tour of the motor pool and company areas

- An informal "hail" lunch with other officers

- Send a "digital tool kit," including a memorandum template and SIR materials

- An introduction to key personnel in the company headquarters with a brief description of their roles

- A walkthrough of the battalion headquarters with a description of how company personnel interact with each staff section

After that, introduce the new platoon leader to their platoon at its worksite. Doing so personally conveys its significance—you are entrusting both the platoon to the lieutenant and vice versa. Inform the platoon that, over the next month or so, the platoon leader's job will be to learn all the necessary skills, and that it will be their job to train If you refuse to on what "right" looks like.

A battalion commander told his lieutenants that his evaluation would place them into one of three categories: The first (and largest) group were those officers who had done a very good job. The next group was for the best performers. But his third and highest rating would go to those who had done the most to help their fellow lieutenants.

The effect on the command climate was dramatic. In contrast to other units, when one of his companies had an inspection, every lieutenant in the battalion would converge to ensure the company was ready."[116]

How the battalion commander shapes their command climate will greatly affect your level of responsibility in a lieutenant's professional development.

Once the lieutenant has had time to review the OER Support Forms (not more than two weeks), bring them in for their initial counseling, and go over the following subjects: [117]

- Company mission, and how they fit into the battalion and the company

- The company's biggest problems and challenges

- The lieutenant's personal and profession goals

- How the lieutenant should conduct their NCO's initial counseling.

- Explain your expectations of them, and assign a reading list of relevant regulations and DA Pamphlets. Set a date to have report back on what they learned about the commander's responsibilities

[116] *Muddy Boots Leadership*, by John Chapman, p52-53
[117] AR 623-3 §3-6a(1), 31 March 2014

At this point, the lieutenant should be able to draw up their own OER Support Form using the Evaluations Entry System[118] and submit it for your review. Pending your approval, they are ready to conduct their own initial counseling with their NCO by the end of their first 30 days.[119]

In the second month, a new lieutenant build professionalism by performing common tasks.

- Conduct a platoon formation inspection

- Conduct a barracks walkthrough and inspect rooms

- Submit ORB revisions to the S-1

- Learn the dispatch cycle and describe everyone's role in the process, by name

- Attend staff/training meetings

- Submit an SIR

- Write a Memorandum For Record

- Read an 026 Deadline Report

- Watch an Article 15 proceeding

- Review standing operating procedures for all sections

- Provide a back-brief from the assigned reading on the commander's responsibilities

- Inventory platoon equipment and assign all items and BII down to supervisors

- Participate in the monthly cyclic inventory

---

[118] https://evaluations.hrc.army.mil/
[119] AR 623-3 §2-12b, 31 March 2014

- Contact the key custodian and develop a lock and key tracker for all platoon equipment

- Review an NCOER

- Establish counseling standards for the platoon

- Review a leave packet

- Create a leader's book with their NCO

At the end of the second month, sit down with the lieutenant, their NCO, and the first sergeant to go over what tasks were accomplished. Provide feedback on what you've seen and heard. If the lieutenant has done well, congratulate the platoon on how well they've trained their platoon leader. This form of investiture will build the platoon's *esprit de corp* and will help change their perspective of the lieutenant from "trainee" to a true "platoon leader."

> *"A new lieutenant is a precious thing.... Don't take advantage of him, but train him, correct him when he needs it (remembering that diplomacy is part of your job description), and be ready to tell the world proudly that he's yours.*
>
> *If you are ashamed of him, maybe it's because you've neglected him or failed to train him properly. Do something about it. Show a genuine concern that he's learning the right way instead of the easy way. But be careful not to undermine his authority or destroy his credibility. Remember that order and counter-order create disorder...."*
> — 1SG Jeffrey J. Mellinger, "Open Letters to Three NCOs," 1989

Beginning with their third month, the lieutenant should further their skills set with the following:

- Run a weapons range
- Oversee an APFT
- Perform quarterly counseling of rated NCOs and supervise junior NCO counseling
- Investigate a commander's inquiry (they will always mess up the first one, so do this early and give remember—it's for training)
- Take on an additional duty (such as Safety Officer)
- Attend a battalion staff meeting
- Update their OER Support Form for quarterly counseling
- Complete an online course (such as container inspector or unit armorer) to broaden knowledge
- Recommend an award
- Develop company staff/training meeting slides
- Observe a promotion board
- Write an Operation Order
- Develop a schedule of evaluations and awards and track progress
- Revise an SOP
- Conduct a reenlistment interview
- Draft their NCO's quarterly performance counseling
- Conduct a home visit
- Present a brown-bag lunch professional development topic to the company officers
- Present a Friday safety brief
- Attend a professional school (one that can go on their ORB)

With a clear vision of what a lieutenant should be able to do, your officer development program becomes much more manageable. Having assigned clear responsibilities, authority to carry them out, visibility on the unit's problems, and the training to handle them, you can complete the circle and hold lieutenants accountable.

When it's time to do the quarterly counseling, compare their performance with the above expectations. You will no doubt have plenty of material to reference in future evaluations.

The Senior Lieutenant

Not every company in the Army has an executive officer in their Modified Table of Organization and Equipment (MTOE). In many cases (almost exclusively in logistics), companies are instead assigned *operations* officers.

The difference is merely semantics; it's the kind of work you give them that will affect their development. An executive officer is primarily concerned with resource management and administration—company headquarters work. An operations officer would focus on maintenance, support missions, and troops-to-task ratios to fill operations orders.

However you choose to utilize your senior lieutenant, you need to bring them in on decisions and explain your decision-making rationale. When you go on leave, they'll be the one to step into your shoes. It only makes sense to spend a few more lunch hours with them.

Staff Rides

Staff rides are the Army version of grade school field trips. As an element of professional development, they offer a chance to get out of the office and appreciate historical sites.

Once a quarter or so, assign someone to plan out a staff ride. That person should present a 10-15 minute briefing about its relevance to the Army today. That way, on the day of the visit, everyone can appreciate the significance of the visit.

For example, while I was in command in Korea, my company visited the Geoje Island POW camp, the site of a North Korean and Chinese prisonerof-war riot in 1951 that captured the U.S. brigadier general commanding the camp. Participants came away with a greater understanding of the Korean War and an appreciation of the U.S. Army's role in defending the peninsula.

If the focus of the event is training, it's possible that mission funds may be used. Contact the S-4 to confirm.

Counseling NCOs

For a new lieutenant, counseling their platoon sergeant can be an intimidating task. Nevertheless, every NCO in the company is required to be counseled on a quarterly basis, including the first sergeant (hint, hint).[120]

The process is exactly the same as it is for officers, so the best training you can give to a lieutenant is to adhere to Army regulation yourself and counsel them on time. Yet if a lieutenant or NCO cannot think of what to counsel a subordinate on, tell them to start with the following:

- Description of the role of the NCO—being an example, conducting day-to-day operations, training soldiers, looking after soldiers and families, and maintaining equipment.[121]

- Assignment of responsibilities that fit into the senior's responsibilities. In the case of a platoon leader, the platoon sergeant will be the only person they immediately supervise, so deciding who to assign tasks to won't be difficult.

- Comparison of the last quarter's performance against expectations.

- Areas to improve that are in keeping with the subordinates' goals. It could be pursuing higher education, applying for an Army program, or attending a course.

---

[120] AR 623-3, §2-12d(2), 31 March 2014
[121] AR 600-20 §2-18, 6 November 2014

- Following the counseling, the rated NCO should update their DA Form 2166-8-1 support form in the Evaluations Entry System so that the senior can reference accomplishments when writing the NCOER.

Conclusion

The responsibility to take care of soldiers is among the most serious and comprehensive duties a commander has to coordinate. In fact, your performance in this matter will probably be the only thing that anyone will ever remember about your time in command.

Your officers, NCOs, and soldiers will not long remember how you did in your inventories, how well maintained the motor pool was, or how quickly you were able to sign their leave forms. If they remember anything about you at all, it will be because you cared for them.

When you think you cannot find the time to do this—to visit the staff duty runner on Christmas or the CQ desk in New Year's Eve, to stop by the hospital when you have to develop the Quarterly Training Brief, or to check on the family with the troublesome kids—remember these words from GEN Colin Powell:

"Leadership is the art of accomplishing more than the science of management says is possible."

The following document for this chapter is available online:

1. Example Storyboard

View available documents at: asktop.net/mocc

Password: 88YEZX9

THE HAMMER

> *"Discipline can only be obtained when all officers are so imbued with the sense of their awful obligation to their men and to their country that they cannot tolerate negligence."—General George S. Patton*

As the company commander, you are responsible for the good order and discipline of your unit. This is a double-edged responsibility—on one hand, you must enforce policies and Army regulations; on the other, you are obligated to respect the rights of those under your authority.[1] The goal is to foster a healthy command climate that accepts diversity, encourages innovation, and preserves personal rights while also observing rank structure and maintaining Army standards.

As you first take command, you may wonder what kinds of events necessitate a call to the brigade legal team. To keep yourself on the straight and narrow, call the JAG office if you have any of the following situations:[2]

1. You receive a report that a soldier has committed a criminal offense
2. You intend to appoint an investigating officer
3. You will conduct a search of a soldier's quarters

[1] Commander's Legal Handbook 2015, §2-2
[2] Commander's Legal Handbook 2015, Preface 2. This list is not exhaustive.

4. You are considering adverse action on a soldier
5. You want to initiate non-judicial punishment under the UCMJ
6. You receive an allegation of family non-support or debt-collection
7. You will conduct a fundraiser or otherwise collect money (for FRG or a hail & farewell)

Notice the majority of these situations involve the possibility of soldier misconduct. As you consider your range of disciplinary options, close communication with the legal team will help you manage your multiple and sometimes competing roles.

The keys are *proportionality* and *neutrality*—matching the proper disciplinary action to the severity of the offense, without prejudice. Unlike civilian authorities, Army commanders can simultaneously act as prosecutor, defense attorney, judge, and jury in disciplinary proceedings. To make sure you get things right, you must have the wisdom to apply the right action to the right situation.

There are six types of disciplinary actions that commanders can take:

1. Corrective
2. Discretionary
3. Administrative
4. Non-judicial punishment
5. Bars to continued service
6. Separation

The next section reviews each type of action and describes when each is most applicable.

Corrective

At the company level, corrective actions focus on fixing behaviors before they develop into larger issues. Successful actions correct the problem without any long-term negative impact on a soldier's career.

On The Spot Corrections

If a soldier appears in an improper uniform, is late to formation, fails to maintain their living space, or has buttons undone on their uniform, the deficiency should be corrected immediately. No one should be above such corrections, from a private who accidentally switched their name and "Army" tags to a lieutenant colonel with their hands in their pockets.[3]

However, this should always be done considerately, and with the goal in mind to further the professionalism of the Army.[4]

Counseling

Disciplinary counseling may be oral or written, but for all intents and purposes, only the written ones count. Oral counseling may be appropriate for the first correction of a minor deficiency. However, on the second occurrence it should be written. If the NCO or soldier is later recommended for further disciplinary action, properly completed counseling statements will be important.

Good disciplinary counseling is the foundation upon which later actions can be built. If forced to pursue that path, a number of questions will come up: Was the deficiency recorded on a DA Form 4856, Developmental Counseling? How did the soldier respond? Did the counselor follow up by completing Section IV—Assessment of the Action Plan? A complete record of developmental counseling statements will be permit a greater range of options later on.

PRO: Simplest step in correcting a recurring deficiency. First step towards more serious action, if required at a later date.

CON: Many NCOs either don't feel confident in their writing abilities or don't feel it's worth the time.

---

[3] AR 670-1 §3-6a(3), 10 April 2015
[4] AR 600-20 §4-6b, 6 November 2014

Mitigation: Have the first sergeant inspect a sample of the counselings done each month, provide feedback (both positive and corrective), and conduct periodic NCOPDs to build writing skills.

> *"Regardless of age or grade, soldiers should be treated as mature individuals. They are men engaged in an honorable profession and deserve to be treated at such."—GEN Bruce Clarke*

Extra Training (also known as Extra Instruction)

Extra training is most appropriate when soldiers have been negligent. Did the soldier miss a deadline-able fault on their vehicle during PMCS? Have them stay late and practice on other vehicles. Did an NCO neglect one of their duties? Have them write a two-page paper about on the relevant regulation.

What's important is to have the training match the deficiency. If a soldier is late, it doesn't make sense to have them do push-ups. Have them show up earlier. This may inconvenience the supervising NCO, but intelligent correction is a hallmark of good leadership.[5]

In the past, physical exercise was frequently imposed to correct deficiencies in other areas, but this is now discouraged. Present guidelines recommend no more than five repetitions in one of ten exercises when physical exercise is used as corrective training.[6]

PRO: Soldiers are often more responsive when their free time is taken.

CON: Supervisors may not want to invest their own free time into correcting soldiers.

Mitigation: Consult the first sergeant to develop appropriate techniques for extra training.

---

[5] AR 27-10 §3-3c, 11 May 2016
[6] FM 7-22 §5-15, 26 October 2012

Denial of Off-post Privileges

Commanders may deny soldiers in the barracks the privilege to leave post. Given the value soldiers place on weekend freedoms, this can be a very effective check on misconduct. To ensure no one sneaks off post unnoticed, though, you'll need to appoint someone who can check the post entrance logs. Note that this is different from restriction, which is an element of non-judicial punishment.

PRO: Highly effective, and only requires a counseling statement and an appointment letter. Can also be used to move off-post residents

CON: If used too often and for too long, it can affect command climate

Mitigation: Limit denials to short periods at first, and consider UCMJ later

Administrative Reprimands

A letter of reprimand is basically a counseling in memorandum format, and may be filed locally or administratively entered into a soldier's Official Military Personnel File (OMPF) with the proper notation.[7] General Officers use Memoranda of Reprimand (GOMORs) to subtly end the careers of senior leaders, but they can also be used as a discreet version of an Article 15 for recording misconduct.

PRO: Reprimands offer a way to record misconduct without matters becoming highly visible.

CON: When pursuing a chapter for patterns of misconduct, reprimands are not as strong as Article 15s.

Mitigation: Administrative reprimands are particularly good for recording a victim's collateral misconduct, e.g. a sexual assault case where the victim had been drinking underage. In this situation, an expedited transfer may prevent UCMJ action, but a reprimand can still be applied.

---

[7] AR 27-10 §3-3b(2), 11 May 2016

Rehabilitative Transfers

There may be times a soldier hasn't done anything big enough to merit a separation, but their NCO support channel is just plain tired of dealing with them. In these cases, a rehabilitative transfer to a different unit may be in order. The first sergeant may be able to move the soldier to a different unit where they can start over.

PRO: Good for soldiers who've had trouble adjusting but are not lost causes

CON: Other units may not want a trouble case, and the MOS has to align with the gaining unit

Mitigation: First sergeants from other units may be willing to trade personnel in the right circumstances

"Good leadership promotes professionalism—a renaissance of standards, involving quality of life, service, discipline, and total commitment to our Army and the United States of America."—MG Albert Akers

Discretionary

Discretionary actions look to correct or prevent issues in ways that do not affect a soldier's career, though they may significantly impact them in the short term. Communicate with the battalion commander if you intend to utilize any of these methods.

Denial of Allowance for Quarters

Soldiers in the rank of E6 and above are normally permitted to live in off-post housing and receive basic allowance for quarters. However, this privilege can be revoked.

PRO: Forcing someone to live on post will enable greater control

CON: This is a drastic measure that will negatively affect a soldier's dignity

Mitigation: It may be the best way to help someone who is considering suicide or is threatened by domestic violence. Depending on which state you are located in, victims of domestic violence may not be able to immediately cancel a lease. As a company commander, you may be able to step in and order a lease termination.

Suspend Driving Privileges

Soldiers or family members with enough traffic violations may have their driving privileges revoked by the garrison commander. As the company commander, you have this authority as well.

PRO: Suspending this privilege may head off a more serious future problem

CON: Responsibility to transport a soldier is transferred to their squad or section, and you cannot demand that soldiers surrender their keys (this would be confiscation).

Mitigation: Changing the soldier's duties or schedule may help reduce the impact of such a decision.

Eviction from On-post Housing

Soldiers and family members who cause problems in on-post housing may be evicted and forced to live off-post. An allowance for housing may be denied at the commander's discretion. In overseas locations, an Early Return of Dependents (EROD) at government expense may also be possible, but is not guaranteed.

PRO: This is a last resort for families who cannot manage their children or relationships with neighbors.

CON: Families may have problems transitioning depending on their finances

Mitigation: Coordinate with the Family Advocacy Program and NCO support channel to prevent recurring issues so that this does not become the garrison commander's preferred option

Bar to Entry on Installations

Spouses who create a disruptive atmosphere within the unit may be banned from the installation. In one instance, a brigade commander's wife had created such a toxic climate within the Family Readiness Group that she was banned from any contact with the FRG and the rest of the brigade.[8]

PRO: Banning a spouse can help reduce unit contacts with a toxic element

CON: Stopping all contact may not prevent another family problem from surfacing later

Mitigation: Keep a close watch on the FRG. No one should wear your rank but you. If the problem is with a particular leader, reduce that spouse's role before it gets to this point.

> *"You do not wake up in the morning a bad person. It happens by a thousand tiny surrenders of self-respect to self-interest."—Robert Brault*

Administrative

Administrative disciplinary actions can have a significant impact on a soldier's career in the long term, but may be necessary to protect the Army's interests. Each of these situations requires a good record of counseling statements to justify the action you decide to take.

---

[8] http://www.militarytimes.com/story/military/archives/2013/03/27/commander-s-wife-banned-from-brigade/78534596/

Removal from Promotion List

Certain situations require removal from the promotion list.[9] However, when a soldier receives a memorandum of reprimand, has been barred, or has been punished under UCMJ Article 15, a commander has the option to recommend that a soldier's name be removed from an approved promotion list.[10] This decision should not be automatic; rather, the soldier's conduct before and after any punishment must be considered. Before sending a removal action to the military personnel office for action, the soldier must be allowed time to respond in writing, and the opinions of third parties may be included.[11]

PRO: Removal from the promotion list will send a strong message throughout the formation.

CON: Even the regulation itself urges caution, as this has far-reaching, long-lasting effects on a solder.

Mitigation: This may be a good measure to implement if the soldier fails to make sufficient progress following an initial infraction.

Suspension/Relief for Cause

For leaders, there are two occasions when relief is necessary—either someone has committed a single, large offense, or they've made a thousand small mistakes that destroy their trustworthiness. An NCO or officer who is suspected of committing an ethical violation must be suspended immediately, pending the results of an investigation. Communicate with the battalion commander if you receive any allegation to this effect.

Relief may also be in order when a soldier in a key position (such as supply sergeant or armorer) has performed poorly over a period of time, despite numerous corrective efforts. However, there are a few limitations.

[9] AR 600-8-19 §7-44, 18 December 2015
[10] AR 600-8-19 §7-45b and c, 18 December 2015. This is a change from the 2011 version.
[11] AR 600-8-19 §7-45f, 18 December 2015

Relief in the first thirty days of a rating period requires a general officer's waiver (even if it's the 13th month they've been in the position).[12] This will typically result in the soldier being moved, rather than relieved. And relief of an NCO from an ad hoc position, such as "training NCO" will require a good record of counseling statements showing how expectations were clearly set and that the soldier failed to meet them.

PRO: Suspension, pending an investigation, is a fairly simple matter when an ethical violation is credibly suspected.

CON: Relief in other circumstances will require a good record of counseling statements showing that rehabilitative efforts have failed.

Mitigation: Be sure to communicate relief decisions with the battalion commander well beforehand.

> *"The commander stands for the virtues of wisdom, sincerity, benevolence, courage, and strictness."—Sun Tzu*

Poor Evaluation

If an NCO or officer has committed an ethical violation, it should be recorded on their evaluation.[13] Poor evaluations can be substantiated through negative counseling statements, and help the Army identify those who are not good candidates for future retention.

PRO: A poor evaluation will help the Army determine who should not be promoted

CON: A proper paper trail is required (which is why giving a merely mediocre evaluation is much much easier.) Also, the benefit to the Army is long term, but the problem is "right now."

---

[12] AR 623-3 §3-55, 4 November 2015
[13] AR 623-3 §3-25, 4 November 2015

Mitigation: Quarterly counseling statements are critical "status checks" to provide to poor performers. A bad evaluation should never be a surprise.

Administrative Reduction

A soldier or NCO who is convicted by a civil court must be considered for reduction in rank.[14] In addition, NCOs may be considered for reduction if they cannot perform duties and responsibilities commensurate of their rank and MOS after being in their position for 90 days. Patterns of conduct or negligence that show the NCO lacks the abilities and qualities expected of their rank and experience are sufficient to convene a reduction board.

While you may be the convening authority for junior enlisted soldier reductions, the battalion commander chairs the boards for sergeants and staff sergeants.[15]

PRO: Reductions following civil convictions send a strong message that public misconduct will not be tolerated.

CON: Reductions for inefficiency or negligence are rarely the fault of the NCO alone, and may not address the root problem.

Mitigation: Proving negligence is best done through a series of good counseling statements.

> "Physical bravery is the baseline, not the great achievement. Moral, ethical, and professional bravery is less common and often more difficult. Leaders casually pledge their lives for an ideal, but refuse to endanger their career, evaluation report, or friendship over such an issue."—John Chapman, Muddy Boots Leadership

---

[14] AR 600-8-19 §10-3a, 18 December 2015
[15] AR 600-8-19 Table 10-1, 18 December 2015

Suspension of Security Clearance

Commanders may determine, on the basis of initial derogatory information, whether it is in the interests of national security to suspend a soldier's security clearance. Among the more common actions that would impact the commander's decision are disregard for public law, dishonest conduct, acts that indicate poor judgment, and episodic use of intoxicants to excess.[16]

At the point an allegation involving moral, ethical, or legal misconduct becomes credible, submit the DA Form 5248 to the S-2 as an initial report and follow up as the situation develops.

PRO: This measure allows commanders to control the amount of damage that can be done by embittered soldiers.

CON: Soldiers generally have security clearances because they need them for work, so it's not good for minor infractions. It also sends the message, "I don't trust you."

Mitigation: Like removal from a promotion list, save this for a second act of misconduct.

MOS Reclassification

Soldiers whose security clearances have been revoked must have their military occupational specialties (MOS) reclassified. This is also true for soldiers in highly visible fields who fail to maintain the highest standards of personal behavior and performance of duty, such as recruitment.[17]

PRO: This will effectively move a poor performer out of the unit.

CON: Can only be done by a field grade officer

---

[16] AR 380-67 §8-3 and §2-4, 24 January 2014
[17] AR 601-280 §9-7a, 31 January 2006 and AR 614-200 §3-19a(4), 26 February 2009

Mitigation: As a company commander, this is merely a recommendation you can make. The battalion command team will likely already be tracking this kind of situation.

Non-Judicial Punishment

The Uniform Code of Military Justice (UCMJ) lists numerous articles under which a soldier can receive punishment by court-martial. However, rather than go through lengthy proceedings for each offense, the Army empowers commanders to impose non-judicial punishment (NJP). As a company commander, you should be familiar with all the articles, but the vast majority of incidents will be the results of misconduct.

Preliminary Inquiry and Flag

If you receive an allegation and there isn't any evidence yet, the first step for a commander is to conduct a preliminary inquiry. This step, also called a "commander's inquiry," is to confirm that an offense was indeed committed and determine who was involved.[18]

At this stage, if you believe that a particular soldier has probably committed an offense, initiate a flag on the soldier using DA Form 268. Notify them in writing via a DA Form 4856 that you will conduct an informal investigation and are considering non-judicial punishment.[19] These two forms must be forwarded to the S-1 so they can mark the soldier's record brief appropriately; it should take no longer than a day.

The flag code will depend on the strength of evidence and the nature of the offense. If you learn of the offense through CID, then Code "M" is most appropriate. Alcohol related offenses, including underage drinking, on-duty impairment, and drunk and disorderly conduct (which would require an ASAP referral) fall under Code "V." Complex investigations may merit a Code "L." If no other code is appropriate, use the one for adverse

---

[18] AR 27-10 §3-14, 11 May 2016
[19] AR 600-8-2 Figure B-1, 11 May 2016

action, Code "A."[20] If you are not sure which code is most appropriate, discuss the issue with your S-1.

Be careful to review the flag report at the beginning of the month and update flag statuses. Careers have been ended because of commanders' neglect in this area.

> Don't develop or publicize any policy that predicts what disciplinary action you will take in a given situation. Not only will it limit your ability to accept extenuating/mitigating circumstances and expose you to charges of favoritism, but unlawful command influence is itself prohibited under Article 37 of the UCMJ.

Informal Investigations

As a company commander, you can direct an *informal investigation*.[21] Informal investigations offer a high level of flexibility and allow you to appoint an investigating officer.

When appointing an investigating officer, clearly state the allegation and the scope of their investigation. Provide any relevant materials you've collected so far, as well as a list of specific questions to answer and key people to interview. Also, specify the timeline they have to complete their report. The JAG office can provide a template for the appointment memorandum.[22]

The investigating officer should visit the JAG office to develop their investigation strategy before they begin, and feel free to check in with you as needed. At the conclusion of the investigation, the investigator should submit all materials to the JAG office for legal review. Once approved, the investigator should provide you with digital and printed copies of the report.

---

[20] AR 600-8-2 §2-2, 11 May 2016
[21] AR 15-6 §2-1a, 2 October 2006. By comparison, formal investigations resemble boards of inquiry and can only be ordered by a colonel or higher.
[22] Commander's Legal Handbook 2015, §15-E

Conducting an investigation is a part of a lieutenant's professional development. Even if you have a fairly straightforward case, assign it so a subordinate can learn from the process. As comedian Steven Wright once noted, 'Experience is something you don't get until just after you need it.'

Allow the lieutenant to stumble through it, but conduct AARs at the end of each stage. After such a learning experience, they'll be much better prepared for a more serious case.

During your time in command, there will be no shortage of opportunities to learn how to handle critical situations. The most common issues usually revolve around the following subject matter:

- **Loss of arms, ammunitions, explosives, or a sensitive item**. This requires an AR 15-6 investigation and a Category 2 serious incident report.[23]

- **Misconduct**. Informal investigations are appropriate for incidents like barracks infractions, fraternization, and command policy violations.[24]

- **Civil or Criminal investigations.** You will need to stay informed on civil and CID investigations, but you won't be the one driving events. More than likely, you will take your cues from your battalion commander.

- **Financial liability investigations of property loss (FLIPLs).** The purpose of these investigations is to determine the cause of a property loss and assign responsibility. Flags are no longer required for subjects of FLIPL investigations.[25]

---

[23] AR 190-11 Appendix E, 5 September 2013; AR 735-5 §13-25, 10 May 2013; and AR 190-45 §8-3, 30 March 2007
[24] Commander's Legal Handbook 2015, §15-B-3
[25] AR 735-5 §13-3 and Table 12-2, 10 May 2013; AR 600-8-2 §2-2, 11 May 2016; Commander's Legal Handbook 2015, Chapter 19

- **Limited use safety accident investigation reports.** A safety investigation must follow each "Army Accident," and be entered in the Report It! website. Class A and B accidents are huge matters, and will require a serious incident report followed by a parallel legal investigation. In these situations, it's important to remember that while the safety report can draw from a legal investigation, legal investigations may not draw information from safety investigations.[26]

- **Line of duty investigations.** These are conducted to determine if a soldier's disease, injury, or death was the result of misconduct or negligence. Company commanders do not initiate these, but they assist the battalion command-appointed investigator with administrative information.[27]

Three Types of Article 15s

If the results of the preliminary or informal investigation lead you to believe a soldier is culpable, you have three options for Non-Judicial Punishment: Summarized, Company grade, and Field grade.

Summarized Article 15. The maximum allowable punishment for summarized proceedings is 14 days of restriction, 14 days of extra duty, an oral admonition, or any combination thereof. Unlike administratively revoking pass privileges, which forbids a soldier from going off-post, **restriction** allows you to limit the soldier's freedom both *on-post and off-post.*

Summarized proceedings are easy to process and even easier to administer. They use DA Form 2627-1, which dispenses with the first reading, and has fewer legal options. (For instance, soldiers do not have the option to request trial by court-martial.) You choose which offenses the

---

26 AR 385-10 §3-8a and §3-10a, 27 November 2013; Commander's Legal Handbook 2015, Chapter 16
27 AR 600-8-4 §1-2 and §2-3, 4 September 2008; Commander's Legal Handbook 2015, Chapter 17

accused is guilty of, and the accused decides whether to appeal or not (they can also defer, if they want more time to decide). Summarized proceedings may only be used on enlisted personnel, and results are filed locally for two years.[28]

If the legal team reports back saying the evidence against the soldier is insufficient, don't intimidate the soldier into accepting an Article 15—they may call your bluff and request a court martial. It's better to settle for corrective discipline than fail to impose any at all.

Company Grade Article 15. The company grade option includes all punishments available in the summarized proceedings (oral reprimand or admonition, 14 days restriction and 14 days additional duty or any combination thereof) plus the following punishment options: a written reprimand, a reduction of one grade for those E-2 to E-4, 7 days correctional custody, forfeiture of 7 days' pay, or any combination thereof.[29] You may also suspend any portion of the punishment as you deem appropriate.

Company grade Article 15s have different filing requirements than summarized proceedings. For soldiers E-4 or below, file the DA Form 2627s locally and retain them for two years. For NCOs, the 2627s must be submitted for entry into their OMPF, and you decide whether to place the 2627 into their restricted file or their performance file. Note that each NCO is only allowed one such document in the restricted OMPF, and that no local filing or restricted folder options are available for sexual offenses.[30]

Field Grade Article 15. These proceedings grant even greater latitude to commanders. If you believe that field grade proceedings are in order, coordinate with your battalion commander. You may have to complete DA Form 5109, Request to Superior to Exercise Article 15 jurisdiction.[31]

28 AR 27-10 §3-16a(1) and f, 11 May 2016
[29] AR 27-10 §3-19, 11 May 2016. See Table 3-1 for a complete list of officer and enlisted punishment options.
[30] AR 27-10 §3-37b, 11 May 2016
[31] AR 27-10 §3-5b, 11 May 2016

The punishment options for a Field grade Article 15 include oral or written admonition/reprimand, 45 days extra duty, 60 days restriction, 30 days correctional custody, reduction in grade one or more ranks for E-2 thru E-4 and reduction of one grade for E-5 thru E-6, loss of ½ month's base pay for two months, or any combination thereof. The commander also has the discretion to suspend any portion of the punishment as they deem appropriate.

Once you've decided which Article 15 proceedings you want to pursue, consult the battalion commander and begin assembling the packet for the legal team. If the legal team's formal review comes back positive, proceed as soon as possible—unnecessary delays minimize the effectiveness of the punishment, and decrease the likelihood the process will be fair, appropriate, and reasonable.

If the legal team reports that the case is insufficient, either set the UCMJ proceedings aside and choose a different action or look to investigate the matter further. Whatever you decide, do not bluff your soldier into accepting an Article 15—it's unfair to your soldier and subverts the military legal system's integrity.

Legal Review

Legal packets generally consist of the following:

- The DA Form 268 flagging the soldier
- The soldier's flagged record brief
- The evidence (e.g. sworn statements or breathalyzer test results)
- Any DA Form 3881 rights waivers, if the subject(s) made a statement
- A memorandum explaining the situation and the type of Article 15 you are pursuing
- Any policies or regulations that apply, for reference

You can email the documents to the legal team, but be sure to encrypt the email because it contains personal information. Then contact the legal team immediately afterwards to ensure the packet arrived at the appropriate addresses. The legal team will review the case and—if valid—prepare the DA Form 2627/2627-1. Follow up if you haven't heard back from them within a week.

Don't try to make an example of your first few cases—it's neither fair nor effective at deterring future misconduct. It will be enough that you addressed a matter firmly and impartially.

First Reading

With the DA Form 2627, you can conduct the first reading. This consists of the formal notification of charges and a review of the maximum allowable punishment for the type of Article 15 you've chosen.[32] The first sergeant normally performs this function, though you may delegate it to a commissioned officer (you may want to provide them the script).[33] After completing boxes 1 and 2, give a copy of the 2627 to the soldier and allow sufficient time for them to consult the JAG office's defense services.

Hearing

After the soldier has had the chance to consult with counsel, schedule the hearing. A company grade Article 15 hearing is a formal matter, and should be conducted according to script.[34] A soldier's NCO support channel and platoon leader should be present, and the soldier should report with all the proper formalities. If the soldier is unaware of these, the first sergeant should coach them on how to proceed.

---

[32] AR 27-10 §3-18a, 11 May 2016
[33] Commander's Legal Handbook 2015, Chapter 6
[34] AR 27-10 Appendix B, 11 May 2016

The soldier has several choices to make during the hearing. They have the option to request trial by court-martial (which would effectively end the hearing until this can be arranged). They can also request that the hearing be open or closed.

Open proceedings do not require you to hold the proceeding in any other location; it is sufficient to simply open the door to your office (although if you wanted to hold it outside during the last formation of the week you should clear this with your legal advisor). Conversely, a closed proceeding is not open to the public, meaning your office door can stay closed. [35] You retain the final decision either way, and should initial your choice in Box 4a. The soldier may also elect to have a spokesperson present, as well as present relevant evidence in defense, extenuation, and/or mitigation.

At this point, you can ask each person their opinion on the matter, then dismiss the soldier while you weigh the evidence presented and discuss the issue with the NCO support channel and platoon leader. When you make your decision on how you want to proceed, fill in the blanks that set the punishment. Note that you have the option to suspend any part of the punishment, which in itself can often be a powerful deterrent in preventing future misconduct.

The 'just get it done' mentality permeates Army culture, but runs counter to the Army's efforts to build a "profession of arms." You can use informal investigations and UCMJ action to shape your unit's organizational culture, but this will likely require some difficult decisions.

One day a company commander got some disturbing reports about events at the unit's weapon qualification range. Poor planning, insufficient ammunition, and disorderly processes led to an abysmal overall qualification rate. Yet according to the NCO running the event, everything was fine and everyone qualified.

---

[35] AR 27-10 §3-18g(2), 11 May 2016

To learn what went wrong, the commander initiated an informal inquiry. Among the many irregularities the investigation discovered was that the NCO in charge of the range had broken up M249 linked ammunition to use in the M4s.

While the M256's 5.56mm ammunition can physically be used in the M4, the linked ammunition used a different Department of Defense Identification Code (DODIC). As such, no one should ever break the links on M249 ammunition without first clearing it with the unit's Quality Assurance Specialist/Ammunition Surveillance (QASAS). Doing so not only throws off ammunition consumption rates (when any unused ammunition is turned in), but it can also risk soldiers' safety if the Army identifies a problem in those M249 rounds.

As a sergeant first class and an 89B Ammunition Specialist, the NCO knew all this, but nevertheless violated both supply and safety protocols to compensate for their own poor usage estimate.

If you were the company commander, how would you handle this? As an E-7, a company grade Article would allow you to take money and assign extra duty, but not reduce rank. The battalion commander may impose a field grade punishment and issue a memorandum of reprimand, but depending on brigade policy may not even be able to reduce rank. That option may be reserved for the brigade commander, who will doubtlessly be scrutinizing you for your ability to handle issues within your company.

The real issue here is how dedicated you are to the "profession of arms" concept. Would you be willing to recommend the NCO to the brigade commander if it meant a "black eye" for your unit? Or would you try to limit negative perceptions by keeping things "in-house"?

No pressure.

Decision

If you believe that the case against the soldier has not been proven beyond a reasonable doubt, bring the accused back in and announce that you have decided to dismiss the proceeding. Destroy all copes of the DA Form 2627.[36] If, on the other hand, you believe the accused is guilty, then initial the correct box in Item 4a, state the punishment that you have decided, and record that in Item 6 of the 2627. For NCOs you find guilty, decide whether you want the 2627 filed in the performance section or the restricted section, and complete the rest of Item 4.

To conclude the proceeding, advise the soldier of their right to appeal, have them initial their choice in Item 5 and sign at the bottom, and then dismiss the soldier.

Publicizing the Punishment

You may choose to announce the punishment at the next unit formation or redact privacy information and post the 2627 on a unit bulletin board. There are two purposes for this: to deter similar misconduct and preclude perceptions of unfairness.[37]

However, before you do this, you should consider how this can impact the unit's morale, any victim, and the degree to which it will provide a deterrent. Given these factors, it may be sufficient to simply speak to the formation about the importance of doing what's right, both on- and off-duty. Soldiers may not know the particulars of what happened, but they'll know you've addressed it.

---

[36] AR 27-10 §3-18k, 11 May 2016
[37] AR 27-10 §3-22, 11 May 2016

Army Body Composition Program

The Army's Body Composition Program (ABCP) is among the most stringently regulated programs in the Army today. The goal is to maintain uncompromising, high standards for the force while also giving soldiers every reasonable opportunity to comply with those standards.

Before considering a bar to continued service or separation, it's important to understand the steps that lead up to this decision. As a commander, failure to follow the right processes will prevent you from exercising the full range of options you have toward ABCP failures.

Enrollment

Every soldier is required to be screened every six months for compliance with the prescribed body fat standard.[38] Screenings should be done at least seven days before or after an APFT to prevent the screening from interfering with APFT results.[39] If the soldier does not comply with standards, initiate a flag (Code "K") and inform the soldier via a DA Form 4856 counseling statement.[40] This enrolls the soldier in the ABCP.

When building a soldier's ABCP file, you have to prepare for the worst—that the soldier will make no progress and need to be separated in six months. With this in mind, the packet must consist of the following:[41]

1. The initial DA Form 5500/5501 worksheet
2. The signed counseling statement informing the soldier that they will be flagged and enrolled in the ABCP
3. The DA Form 268 flag using Code "K"
4. Your ABCP enrollment memorandum to the soldier (see AR 600-9 Figure 3-1)

---

[38] AR 600-9 §3-2a, 28 June 2013
[39] AR 600-9 §3-4b, 28 June 2013
[40] AR 600-8-2 §2-3c and §2-7, 11 May 2016
[41] AR 600-9 §3-8 and Table 3-1, 28 June 2013

5. The soldier's acknowledgement memo stating that they have completed the mandatory online Move123! training (Figure 3-4). The soldier must complete this within 14 days of the counseling.

6. The memorandum from the soldier's dietician stating the nutrition counseling results (Figure 3-5). The soldier is required to meet with their dietician within 30 days of your counseling.[42] You may also want to provide the soldier with a memorandum to the health care provider stating the reason for the referral.

7. Your request to the health care provider for a medical evaluation (Figure 3-6). Although you can wait on this until the soldier fails the program, it's better to simply do it right away.

8. The health care provider's medical evaluation results (Figure 3-7), and finally,

9. Subsequent monthly DA Form 5500/5501s showing the soldier's progress.[43]

"Every great leader I have known has been a great teacher, able to give those around him a sense of perspective and to set the moral, social, and motivational climate among his followers."
—*ADM James Stockdale*

Monthly Assessments

Soldiers enrolled in the ABCP must receive monthly assessments approximately every 30 days, and are expected to lose either 3 to 8 pounds or 1 percent body fat. Soldiers who meet either of these goals are making "satisfactory progress." Have the first sergeant review the 5500/5501s monthly and brief you on results.

As soon as a soldier has conformed to body composition standards, you must remove them from the program.[44] (Regulations do not permit

[42] AR 600-9 §3-6c, 28 June 2013
[43] AR 600-9 §3-9, 28 June 2013
[44] AR 600-9 Figure 3-8, 28 June 2013

a waiting period.) Note that compliance with weight standards is not enough to be released—individuals *must* meet the body fat standards.[45]

Program Successes

Though soldiers can be released from the ABCP, they are not out of the woods yet. A subsequent body composition failure within 12 months requires another flag and a medical evaluation. Without a qualifying "temporary medical condition," you must initiate either a bar to continued service or separation.

If the soldier fails to maintain standards between the 12th and 36th month following their release, you must initiate the ABCP again, and—if there is no qualifying temporary medical condition—enroll them in the ABCP again. This time, however, they will have only 90 days to complete the program.[46]

Program Failures

Those who do not exhibit satisfactory progress 1) in two consecutive monthly assessments, 2) after three non-consecutive assessments, or 3) are still on the program after 6 months, are considered program failures. If you haven't already requested a medical evaluation, it's mandatory at this point.

If there is no qualifying temporary medical condition, you must initiate either a bar to continued service or separation. Counsel the soldier on your decision in writing and initiate the process.[47]

> *"The nail that sticks up gets hammered down."* (出る杭は打たれる)
> — *Japanese Proverb*

---

[45] AR 600-9 §3-13a, 28 June 2013
[46] AR 600-9 §3-14, 28 June 2013
[47] AR 600-9 §3-12d, 28 June 2013

Enforcing Compliance

The ABCP flag is a *transferable* flag, meaning that it is possible for a soldier do a permanent change of station (PCS) while still enrolled in the ABCP. Possible, yes, but undesirable—it's better to fix a soldier's issues while they are with the unit than pass them on for someone else to deal with.

You can prevent an ABCP enrollee from a permanent change of station by instituting a bar to continued service early in the ABCP timeline, rather than waiting until program failure. This measure will not only retain the soldier at the unit the issue is fully dealt with, but will also force a separation if progress is not made by the six month point. Depending on the duty station, this can be quite a powerful incentive ("How long would you like to stay here at Fort Drum, soldier?").

Bars to Continued Service

Soldiers who do not meet Army standards deserve to be notified so that they can overcome their deficiencies. Yet the Army also deserves a method of recourse against soldiers who cannot comply with basic standards of service.

The purpose of a bar to continued service is to place the soldier on notice that his or her continued service may not be in the Army's best interest.[48] If a barred soldier cannot correct their deficiency by the sixth month, the soldier must be separated.

Untrainable or unsuitable soldiers, two-time APFT failures, those who cannot complete a mandatory Family Care Plan, and those who consistently fail to abide by military expectations are prime candidates for bars. For instance, a specialist who meets minimum standards for their current rank but lacks the potential to be an NCO may be deemed untrainable and considered for a bar.[49]

---

[48] Army Directive 2016-19 Enclosure 1, §4c, 26 May 2016
[49] Army Directive 2016-19 Enclosure 1, §8-4, 26 May 2016

After consulting the first sergeant and the soldier's first line supervisor, a company commander's next step in barring a soldier will be to confer with the battalion commander as the approving authority. Once you've "pre-cleared" the bar, work with the career counselor or retention NCO to draw up the DA Form 4126.

To illustrate the process, consider a soldier who consistently failed to qualify on their assigned weapon, despite remedial training. Bring the soldier in, counsel them on their deficiency, and inform them that you are recommending a bar until they can qualify. The soldier will have an opportunity to provide a statement within seven days, after which time the career counselor will submit the 4126 to the command sergeant major for the battalion commander's signature. With the approval authority's signature, the soldier must be counseled again that the bar has been approved, the soldiers will be flagged, and they will have their first review in 90 days.[50]

If that soldier is able to qualify on their weapon within 90 days, submit a recommendation that the battalion commander lift the bar. If approved, counsel the soldier that the bar has been lifted, and lift the flag as well. If, however, 90 days have passed and that soldier is still not able to qualify, conduct the first review (with the first sergeant and career counselor present).

Again, if that soldier is able to qualify in the next three months, then ask for the bar to be lifted. Yet if the deficiency remains, it's time to begin separation proceedings.[51]

---

[50] Army Directive 2016-19 Enclosure 1, K-4, 26 May 2016
[51] AR 635-200 §1-47, 6 June 2005

Separations

"Soldiers who do not conform to required standards of discipline and performance and soldiers who do not demonstrate potential for further military service should be separated in order to avoid the high costs in terms of pay, administrative efforts, degradation of morale, and substandard mission performance."[52]

A decision to separate a soldier is not to be taken lightly. As the commander you owe it to the Army to attempt all reasonable rehabilitative measures before pursuing separation. Nonetheless, sometimes your best judgment will be that it's time for a soldier to part ways.

With that said, separations are differentiated by the AR 635-200 chapters that cover them. For instance, a "chapter 13" separation is for unsatisfactory performance. A "chapter 9" is for a substance abuse program failure. Those who cannot complete an adequate family care plan are separated under chapter 5.[53]

For each chapter, there are two procedures: the notification procedure for those with less than six years of service, and an administrative board for those with more than six years. The two procedures have different processing times—15 working days for notification versus 50 working days for the administrative board. The administrative board is longer because it requires a medical examination, time to consult with counsel, and a legal review.

As a company commander, your first step to processing a separation packet is to contact the legal team. Review the Summary of Separation Actions from the Commander's Legal Handbook with the legal team to determine the most applicable chapter for the situation and whether the actions taken so far meet the required threshold for that action.[54] Notice that many chapters require a record of counseling statements (with the

---

[52] AR 635-200 §1-1c3(b), 6 June 2005
[53] AR 635-200 §5-18, 6 June 2005
[54] Commander's Legal Handbook 2015, §28-H

Assessment section complete) forewarning the soldier that separation is a potential consequence of non-compliance.[55]

With this information, you can present your recommendation to the battalion commander. Depending on the particular chapter and the characterization of the discharge, they may be able to adjudicate this themselves. If not, it will require approval by the commanding general.

From this point forward, you would take your cues from the legal team. You may need to provide a commanding officer's report (as required by unsatisfactory performance and patterns of misconduct[56]), but the most difficult part—the counseling documentation—will have already been done.

Conclusion

Instilling discipline into those who cannot do it for themselves is one of the greatest challenges of command. When the Army was growing to meet the challenges of the Global War on Terror, discipline was more lenient. Now that we face a more selective environment, commanders must take a harder look at who should be allowed to collect a government paycheck versus those that should enter the civilian workforce.

Commanders must decide what honest mistakes are acceptable and what situations require more serious action up to and including separation. It is also important for a commander to understand the unintended consequences of their actions. Sometimes these consequences can set into motions a series of events that the commander never intended and cannot control. Take your time and think through the issue, your options, and seek advice from those who have experience in the situation you are confronting.

Regardless, commanders must always bear in mind that " awful obligation to both the country and their soldiers" that General Patton referred to, as it is found in Title 10, U.S. Code §3583:[57]

---

[55] AR 635-200 §1-16b, 6 June 2005
[56] AR 635-200 Figure 2-5, 6 June 2005
[57] Also found in AR 600-20 §1-5c(4)(d), 6 November 2014

"All commanding officers and others in authority in the Army are required—

1. to show in themselves a good example of virtue, honor, patriotism, and subordination;

2. to be vigilant in inspecting the conduct of all persons who are placed under their command;

3. to guard against and suppress all dissolute and immoral practices, and to correct, according to the laws and regulations of the Army, all persons who are guilty of them; and

4. to take all necessary and proper measures, under the laws, regulations, and customs of the Army, to promote and safeguard the morale, the physical well-being, and the general welfare of the officers and enlisted persons under their command or charge."

TRAINING MANAGER

> "Do essential things first. There is not enough time for the commander to do everything. Each commander will have to determine wisely what is essential... Nonessentials should not take up time required for essentials."—GEN Bruce Clarke[1]

Previous chapters have focused on caring for soldiers and stewardship of Army resources. Yet there is an ever greater responsibility that our leaders place on us—to win our nation's wars. At the company level, we are responsible for building deployment-ready units within the guidelines of each company's Mission Essential Task List (METL).[2]

In your role as the unit's training manager, you must be able to understand and implement the items below:

1. Develop and present your unit's Quarterly Training Brief (QTB) to the brigade commander (for long term planning)

2. Conduct training meetings and plan training events (for the medium term), and

3. Track training completion rates through the Defense Training Management System (DTMS) software (for the short term)

---

[1] As quoted in FM 25-101 Battle-focused Training, 1990, §2-1
[2] Divisional units are typically organized at the battalion level, but units outside the brigade combat team structure are organized at the company level.

To effectively manage the training schedule on top of all the other programs in previous chapters, you're also going to need good time management skills. This includes the development of effective battle rhythms and incorporating Physical Readiness Training (PRT) into the daily training schedule.

Quarterly Training Briefs

When planning a unit's training schedule, the Army envisions a battalion using the Military Decision Making Process (MDMP) to methodically analyze and decide which tasks the unit will train on. Afterward, companies receive a synchronized training calendar upon which they can schedule their own events. The full process can be found in the Army Training Network's Leader's Guide to Unit Training Management.[3]

While this battalion-centric approach makes things easier for company commanders, it is not always appropriate for units who are either geographically separated from the parent unit or would deploy independently. In these cases, the process begins with a good understanding—either through training guidance, an order, or a simple conversation with the battalion commander—of what your unit will be expected to do in either a combat or contingency scenario.

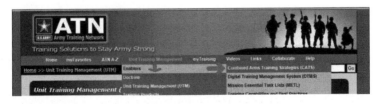

[3] https://atn.army.mil/media/docs/LG_to_UTM_FINAL.pdf

Once you understand the company's mission, you can look through the list of Key Collective Tasks (KCTs) on the Combined Arms Training Strategies (CATS) webpage to see which are most appropriate to focus on.[4] The CATS site provides the KCTs for every unit type, from Acquisitions contracting teams to Transportation watercraft maintenance companies.[5]

The full list of your unit's KCTs is meant to be a training "menu" from which commanders choose their highest priorities. With your KCT list in hand, recommend a training focus to the battalion commander about what the training focus should be over the next coming quarters. Pending their approval, you can take one of two approaches to planning your training calendar.

Developing the Course of Action

The simplest, quickest way to plan training is the "white tower" approach. For this, you sit down with the first sergeant and maybe the executive officer and go over the calendar for the quarter.

Using Steven Covey 's "biggest rocks" method, you fill in the calendar with the highest priority events first (such as a quarterly culminating training event), then add the less important things. Depending on your unit, your priorities might look like this:

1. Training holidays
2. Brigade/battalion training events (such as a sports week)
3. Mandatory group training events (EO, SHARP, seasonal safety, etc.)
4. Cyclic inventory layouts
5. Qualification ranges and preliminary range instruction dates

---

[4] https://atn.army.mil/dsp_CATSviewer01.aspx. ATN > Unit Training Management > Enablers > CATS
[5] You will hear the term "Mission Essential Task List," or METL, used frequently. This is used for assessing readiness in Unit Status Reports (USR), but is less helpful when deciding on a training focus.

6. Scheduled maintenance services (these should be on the training calendar because users will need to be available to assist with the services)

7. Key Collective Task training

8. Low density training (when CBRN, human resources, or supply personnel are meet with their respective battalion staff section NCOICs)

9. Emergency deployment readiness and/or combat load retrieval exercises

10. Newcomers briefings

11. Ceremonies (promotion, retirement, and ETS)

12. Sergeant's Training Time and Warrior Task and Battle Drill training

13. Physical fitness tests and body composition test dates

14. Family Readiness Group meetings

15. Professional development/Warrior Adventure Quest events

The advantage to the "white tower" approach is that—at its conclusion—you have a solid grasp of what events will happen throughout the next three months. And for units with a significant garrison mission (such as headquarters or logistics companies), you may only have one day a week to really *train* anyway. The disadvantage is that you have drawn up a plan that will affect everyone in the unit, but only involved the small circle around you—the rest of the unit is left to simply show up and do what they're told.

> Leadership provides purpose, direction, and motivation. Discipline makes soldiers receptive to instruction and training teaches soldiers what to do and when to do it. In the speed and chaos of battle, leadership can be drowned out. Discipline will maintain unit coherence, but it does not guide. When things get bad—when it's time to take action—soldiers will default to what they have been <u>trained</u> to do.

In their book *Taking the Guidon*, authors Nate Allen and Tony Burgess describe a more dynamic approach to training management. By "crowdsourcing" the unit's training calendar, they were able to draw on the experiences of a wider circle of NCOs and build enthusiasm within the unit. Instead of treating the schedule as merely an end state to be reached, the process becomes a professional development exercise involving multiple levels of company leadership.

To implement this method, begin by reviewing the company-level KCTs for platoon-level leadership, and then explain the planning process to each platoon's leaders. Show them the ATN website and how to access both collective and individual training tasks. If you have a culminating event, establish that at the beginning to provide focus for the unit. Explain the end state you have in mind, and then give them some time to meet with their squad and team leaders to discuss what they think the priorities are.

When you bring the platoon leadership back (either with or without the squad/team leaders), have them present what platoon-level tasks they think should take priority over others. For instance, one of an Infantry Brigade Combat Team Rifle Company's 30 KCTs is "Perform Basic Tactical Tasks—Platoon," which has 19 subordinate tasks.

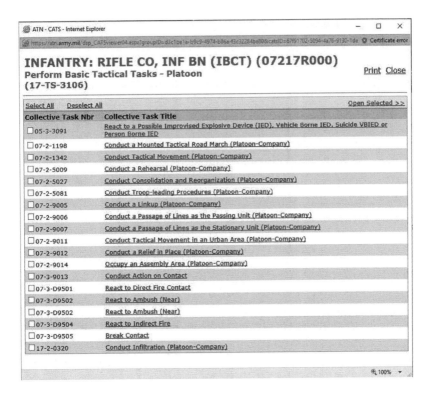

INFANTRY: RIFLE CO, INF BN (IBCT) (07217R000)
Perform Basic Tactical Tasks – Platoon (17-TS-3106)

Print Close

Select All Deselect All   Open Selected >>

Collective Task Nbr	Collective Task Title
☐ 05-3-3091	React to a Possible Improvised Explosive Device (IED), Vehicle Borne IED, Suicide VBIED or Person Borne IED
☐ 07-2-1198	Conduct a Mounted Tactical Road March (Platoon-Company)
☐ 07-2-1342	Conduct Tactical Movement (Platoon-Company)
☐ 07-2-5009	Conduct a Rehearsal (Platoon-Company)
☐ 07-2-5027	Conduct Consolidation and Reorganization (Platoon-Company)
☐ 07-2-5081	Conduct Troop-leading Procedures (Platoon-Company)
☐ 07-2-9005	Conduct a Linkup (Platoon-Company)
☐ 07-2-9006	Conduct a Passage of Lines as the Passing Unit (Platoon-Company)
☐ 07-2-9007	Conduct a Passage of Lines as the Stationary Unit (Platoon-Company)
☐ 07-2-9011	Conduct Tactical Movement in an Urban Area (Platoon-Company)
☐ 07-2-9012	Conduct a Relief in Place (Platoon-Company)
☐ 07-2-9014	Occupy an Assembly Area (Platoon-Company)
☐ 07-3-9013	Conduct Action on Contact
☐ 07-3-D9501	React to Direct Fire Contact
☐ 07-3-D9502	React to Ambush (Near)
☐ 07-3-D9502	React to Ambush (Near)
☐ 07-3-D9504	React to Indirect Fire
☐ 07-3-D9505	Break Contact
☐ 17-2-0320	Conduct Infiltration (Platoon-Company)

🔍 100% ▾

Which of these should be the highest priority? Which is the lowest? As the commander, you could probably make a decent decision by yourself, but by fostering discussion, you instill a greater sense of platoon commitment to the execution.

Although this method is more time consuming, the end product you develop will be the result of your entire company, and sergeants will be able to explain exactly what they are doing and why.[6] More importantly, you will have shown your lieutenants a best practice that can help the Army's next generation of leaders.

---

[6] This fulfills the ideal in AR 350-1 §1-19b, 19 August 2014, where learning objectives (including standards, educational outcomes, and conditions) for each task are understood by all participants.

Presentation

Once you've developed a course of action, you'll submit your plan for approval, first to the battalion commander, then to the brigade commander. This will be one of the few times you will meet face-to-face with your senior rater, so it will be important for you to do well.

As with the Community Health Promotion Councils, find out beforehand what kinds of things are important to your senior rater. Do they value preparation (in which case you may want to write a script), or do they prefer a more casual presentation style?

Ask your fellow commanders and the S-3 about their lessons learned and observations when briefing the boss. Brigade commanders with a penchant for details will look closely at the METL crosswalk and METL assessment slides, so be prepared to justify your assessments of those collective tasks with DTMS records. Others will want high completion percentages in certain Warrior Tasks and Battle Drills, or impactful storyboard summaries from the previous three months of training.

Regardless of the engagement method for the briefs, it is imperative to put your best foot forward during these rare opportunities to interact with your senior rater. This is one of those situations where it truly pays to do your homework. Some will say, "It's not how you start, but how you finish," but the reality is that everything involving your senior rater is a test. Get a copy of the slides from the previous QTB, and design your training around the priorities you see. Finally always review the S-3's slide deck before the presentation—you definitely don't want any "surprises" in front of senior leaders. If you find a discrepancy just before the meeting, attempt to correct it. If this is not possible, make an annotation on your copy and be ready to address it with the boss during your brief.

"A leader is best when people barely know he exists; when the work is done, his aim fulfilled, the people will say, 'We did it ourselves.'"
—Lao Tzu

Training Meetings

While the QTB provides the goal and the overall "sight picture" for your unit's training, the particulars of training are addressed in weekly training meeting. These meetings, which should be entirely separate from your administrative meetings (where you discuss awards, NCO-ERs, and so on) should follow the battalion training meetings by not more than two days.

The training meeting serves four purposes: to assess the previous weeks training (T+1), to coordinate events in the short term (T-1 through T-5), to plan out events in the medium term (T-6 and T-7), and to check on mandatory training. The agenda should be established before your first meeting and repeated every time so that subordinates know what to prepare.

Training meetings should start with a review of the previous week's training, and should address the following issues:

1. What collective and individual tasks (including Warrior Task and Battle Drills) each platoon trained on during the previous week. All certificates, sign-in rosters, and scoresheets should be turned in to the training NCO immediately.
2. What training was planned, but not conducted, and why. If a higher echelon redirected events (i.e. due to a safety stand-down or SHARP briefing), this needs to be noted for a future QTB.
3. Consider whether any retraining is required
4. Review any FRAGOs for updated command guidance or new, superseding missions
5. Update the company's KCT completion tracker and METL assessments

These steps should take no more than 15 minutes.

Next, when reviewing the upcoming events, you'll need to cover:

1. Review weeks T-1 through T-5. Consider any requests for changes to the training plan (such as the NCOIC for the event, the number of tasks to cover, location, or training focus) (30 minutes)
2. Approve the final version of week T-6 and review the draft training schedule for T-7 (15 minutes)
3. Identify major training facilities, assign responsibility for execution, and receive any updates for weeks T-8 through T-21 (10 minutes)
4. Identify any DTMS updates (5 minutes)

All total, the Army envisions that a good training meeting will last about 90 minutes, but if you can get to the point where training meetings last no more than one hour, even better.

"Failure to lock-in training and adhere to published training schedules can ruin the unit's ability to execute effective training. It also creates an atmosphere in which leaders and Soldiers at all levels lose confidence in the [leadership's ability] to ensure training is protected and supported by the chain of command. The message sent by such indiscipline is that training and leader development are not priorities"—Leader's Guide to Training Meetings, December 2013

Training Timeline

Outside of the training meeting, your training management team (comprised of the executive officer, first sergeant, the training NCO, and maybe a junior enlisted assistant) should prepare training according to a set timeline. Week by week, their responsibilities look like this:

- T-13 and beyond: Reserving land and/or major training facilities. . Depending on your location, land for training may have to be arranged far in advance. While this may not be as important in

Fort Hood, it certainly is in Hawaii and Korea, where available land is more limited

- T-12: Identify prerequisite training. For a company level field exercise, platoons should have their squads trained on the individual elements of that field exercise (e.g. Conducting an Attack or React to Indirect Fire) no later than T-4. Utilizing the crawl-walk-run methodology, subordinate units should have in mind the tasks to train on over the next eight weeks. Sergeant's Time Training is the best time for training on basic individual tasks.

- T-11: Refine the plan and distribute the CATS-provided standards for the event to key leaders. "Perform Redeployment Training Activities (Task #55-2-4815)," for example, lists specific tasks for the commander, the training NCO, and unit leaders.

- T-10: Publish a WARNO identifying the training audience, training objectives, location, date, and required resources (such as food and transportation). Also, begin the pre-execution checks.[7] For exercises that involve Master Scenario Event List (MSEL) injects, role players, or special facilities, this is the time to identify installation training agencies who can "train the trainer"

- T-9: Evaluate resource requirements and submit initial resource requests. CATS offers estimates for fuel and ammunition, and vehicle usage rates to provide to the S-3 and S-4 shops.

- T-8: Execute reconnaissance, inspecting the training site for things like sleep areas or environmental hazards.[8] Lock in resources and confirm land reservations with installation.+

---

[7] A more complete list is in *Leader's Guide to Training Meetings*, pages 11 and 30, December 2013

[8] *Leader's Guide to Training Meetings*, page 37, offers a more complete list of questions

- T-7: Publish an operations order for the event, complete with annexes. For field exercises, one of the annexes should be the packing list so that soldiers have time to prepare or replace required gear.

- T-6 If the goal for publication is six weeks out, lock in the training and submit the training schedule to the S-3 for battalion commander approval. Require risk assessments from training leaders and review them to see if the residual risk level requires approval by a higher level command.[9]

- T-5: Complete the tactical plan and supporting products. For a squad training exercise (STX) lane, observer-controller/trainers (OCTs) should be briefed on what their roles will be and given the relevant manuals for the task they'll train.

- T-4: Complete all prerequisite training. By this point, all "train the trainer" tasks are completed, range leader certifications are done, and subordinate levels are ready for the higher tasks (i.e. squads are ready for a platoon event).

- T-3: Conduct rehearsals. Perform a final reconnaissance of the training site to check any changes the weather may have caused and to confirm the convoy route. For an STX, the first sergeant should walk through each lane and review the training plan.[10]

- T-2: Finalize administrative support requirements, confirming any land reservations and wash rack requests. For travel off-post, submit convoy clearance requests and conduct OPFOR rehearsals to ensure participants fully understand their roles. Soldiers should conduct pre-combat checks (PCCs).

---

[9] DA Pam 385-30 Table 4-1, 2 December 2014
[10] *Leader's Guide to Training Meetings,* page 53 has a good checklist.

- T-1: Draw any equipment and supplies, such as training materials and Class V pyrotechnics. Note that while it may seem better to conduct this task earlier, you may have no choice but to wait until this point—pyrotechnics will have to be secured until use, and installation training centers often have frequent requests for their supplies. NCOs execute pre-combat inspections (PCIs).

- T-0: Execute training

Not every step applies to every training event, but this timeline at least provides a guide by which you can set expectations and hold your training team accountable.

Tracking Mandatory Training

All individual unit and collective training must be documented in individual training records utilizing DTMS.[11] Yet of all the things to maintain records on, mandatory periodic training should be the highest priority, as higher echelons may pull these tasks to compare units' completion rates.

To maintain visibility on your mandatory training situation, have your training team check DTMS on the day before each weekly training meeting. In addition to any specific training highlighted in the QTB (such as Warrior Tasks/Battle Drills) it should report the completion rates of the following (see next page):

---

[11] AR 350-1 §3-25d, 19 August 2014. For a list of items that must be included, see §4-4a.

Training	Source	Authority
Operations Security (OPSEC)[1]	Classroom	AR 530-1 §4-2a
Army Values & Ethics[2]	Classroom	AR 600-20
Army Substance Abuse Program (ASAP)[3]	Classroom	AR 600-85 §2-33b
Suicide Prevention	Classroom	AR 600-63 §4-7d
SHARP	Classroom	AR 600-20 §8-7b
Equal Opportunity[4]	Classroom	AR 350-1 G-16
Threat Awareness & Reporting Program (TARP)	Classroom	AR 381-12 §1-6b
Combat Life Saver[5]	Classroom	AR 350-1 G-14a(1)
Domestic violence prevention	Classroom	AR 600-20 §4-22c(2)
Army Physical Fitness Test (semi-annual)	Event	AR 350-1 G-9m(2)
Weapon Qualification (semi-annual)	Event	AR 350-1 Table G-1
Risk Management (JS-US008)[6]	Online	DA Pam 385-30 §
Global Assessment Tool (GAT)	Online	Army Directive 2013-07, Enclosure 2 §3
Antiterrorism (AT) training (JS-US007)	Online	AR 350-1 G-8a
Law of War (ARNJ 7-US033)	Online	AR 350-1 Table G-1
Information Security[7]	Online	AR 380-5 §9-7
SERE 100 (for OCONUS locations, tri-annual)[8]	Online	AR 350-1 G-11d(3)(a)
Combating Trafficking in Persons CTIP) J3T A-US030	Online	AR 350-1 Table G-1
Personnel Recovery (J3O P-US018) and Code of Conduct	Online	AR 525-28 §4-3a

(Footnotes)

[1] Initial training in Level I due within 30 days of arrival at organization, and annually thereafter

[2] Though specified in AR 350-1 G-16, the 4 November 2014 version of AR 600-20 does not mention these.

[3] Four hours annually. This can be conducted in the holding room during urinalysis testing

[4] Equal Opportunity training is often performed quarterly with a focus rotating among Hazing/Bullying, conflict management/resolution, and fraternization.

[5] One soldier per squad required

[6] Exercise of risk management is an ongoing requirement; this online course may be required of supervisors

[7] For those with access to classified/sensitive information

[8] An Isolated Persons form (DD Form 1833) is also required for all overseas travel, but is not considered a training requirement.

Review the training statistics on a weekly basis, and emphasizing the tasks with the lowest percentages. Once your training team gets used to reporting company-wide percentages, have them break it down into platoons, and start looking at what percentages are below 90 percent. Brigades often score companies on a Red-Yellow-Green scale; while the exact percentages may vary, 90 percent is usually the threshold you have to be at to stay green.

At the time of publication, one of the biggest problems with DTMS was the disconnect between DTMS and real-world training events. For example, if you wanted to upload your unit's SHARP training, what task should you upload it as—"SHARP," "SHARP Quarterly Training," or "1st Brigade SHARP Trng"? If the battalion and brigade S-3 shops were not on the same page, they would report on different tasks; one level might report you have a high completion percentage while another said zero. (Or, if you were unlucky, both would say zero).

The dilemma could be solved through the issuance of clear guidance from higher, but brigade S-3s often found themselves in the same position as battalions—they didn't want to issue guidance without word from division. To hedge against a wrong guess, training staff would simply direct units to upload the training stats into all three DTMS tasks.

To save your soldiers from unnecessarily duplicating effort, get clarity on how battalion wants training uploaded. DTMS's flexibility is often a nice feature, but not always.

Tracking Training Preparations

Major (and even minor) training events require weeks of planning and preparation to ensure success. However, training preparation is not like a race with a finish line. It more like a conveyor belt—one event will finish and you'll have another right afterward. Keeping track of everything is a challenge to say the least.

The best way to keep visibility on these tasks is the "Rolling T" method, as described by *Taking the Guidon* author Nate Allen. To do this, have your training team set up three marker boards to look like this:

View on Monday, 3 October 2016								
Board 1								**Remarks**
Week	1	T-0	Oct	3	4	5	6	7	
Week	2	T-1	Oct	10	11	12	13	14	
Week	3	T-2	Oct	17	18	19	20	21	
Week	4	T-3	Oct	24	25	26	27	28	
Board 2								**Remarks**
Week	5	T-4	Nov	31	1	2	3	4	
Week	6	T-5	Nov	7	8	9	10	11	
Week	7	T-6	Nov	14	15	16	17	18	
Week	8	T-7	Nov	21	22	23	24	25	
Week	9	T-8	Nov	28	29	30	1	2	
Board 3								**Remarks**
Week	10	T-9	Dec	5	6	7	8	9	
Week	11	T-10	Dec	12	13	14	15	16	
Week	12	T-11	Dec	19	20	21	22	23	
Week	13	T-12	Dec	26	27	28	29	30	

Each day is filled in with that day's training focus, and key tasks for that week are placed in the Remarks column. Changes to the board should be written in red for quick recognition. At the end of the week, the training team should note the changes and replace the red ink with black so that you can begin fresh the following Monday.

In this example, the Range OIC should complete the installation range certification by the end of T-4 and provide a copy to the training team. Once checked, the training team would write "Cert complete" in red marker.

				31	1	2	3	4	Remarks
Week	5	T-4	Nov	PMCS	PMI	M4 qualification	M249 qualification	Recover / AAR	Check Range OIC cert

As each week passes, the training team updates the "T-#" column, and replaces the dates of the "T+1" week that just passed with the new "T-12" dates. The training team then fills in the training tasks for the newest week. In the previous example, the training team would erase the remarks and put the T-3 task, "2nd Recon, Rehearsal," in that spot.

After four weeks, the boards would look like this:

View on Tuesday, 1 November 2016									
Board 1									**Remarks**
Week	1	T-9	Jan	2	3	4	5	6	
Week	2	T-10	Jan	9	10	11	12	13	
Week	3	T-11	Jan	16	17	18	19	20	
Week	4	T-12	Jan	23	24	25	26	27	
Board 2									**Remarks**
Week	5	T-0	Nov	31	1	2	3	4	
Week	6	T-1	Nov	7	8	9	10	11	
Week	7	T-2	Nov	14	15	16	17	18	
Week	8	T-3	Nov	21	22	23	24	25	
Week	9	T-4	Nov	28	29	30	1	2	

Board 3									Remarks
Week	10	T-5	Dec	5	6	7	8	9	
Week	11	T-6	Dec	12	13	14	15	16	
Week	12	T-7	Dec	19	20	21	22	23	
Week	13	T-8	Dec	26	27	28	29	30	

The Rolling T method requires consistent updates, but it allows for quick assessments and can be easily duplicated in Microsoft Outlook. Doing so will allow your training team to quickly and easily share visibility on training events.

Managing the Battle Rhythm

The Army mandates that DTMS be used to manage unit training.[12] However, training is not the only thing a company needs to track, and DTMS calendars are not always easy to read. To complement the training schedule, you need to establish monthly and weekly battle rhythms that incorporate all the expectations placed on the unit. Here is one example:

Company Battle Rhythm

Quarterly
- Quarterly Training Brief
- Performance counselings
- FRG event
- BN Staff assistance visits

Monthly
- Receive cyclic/SII inventory (by 5th)
- Barracks inspection (first week)
- Monthly reports (due on 10th)
- FRG Newsletter (by the 15th)
- Supply/Maint recons (by the 15th)
- New soldier orientation (3rd Thurs)
- T/I completed cyclic/SII (by 25th)
- Internal inspection (last week)
- Special PRT event

Weekly
- Command maintenance (Mon 0930)
- Award/Evaluation review (Mon 1600)
- High risk review (Tue 0930)
- BN Cmd&Staff mtg (Tue 1030)
- XO Synch (Tue 1500)
- Company Training mtg (Wed 1330)
- Closeout formation (Fri 1600)

Weekly Products
- Schedule for T-6 to BN (Wed 1100)
- SIGACTs/Storyboards (Thu 1200)
- Great soldier nomination (Thu 1200)
- Slide submission (Fri 1100)
- Training closure report (Fri 1600)

[12] AR 350-1 §1-19, 19 August 2014

Like a heartbeat, the battle rhythm sets the pace of your unit's operations. If the unit doesn't already have a clearly defined battle rhythm, draw up one yourself and assign responsibilities. Doing so will help keep common, regular tasks coordinated both well-coordinated and timely.

To develop an accurate battle rhythm, make sure you get either a good initial counseling or thorough initial command inspection back-brief. The Army requires that the initial command inspection be scheduled on the training calendar, and provide "a clear picture of the goals, standards, and priorities for the unit."[13] This may be a difficult thing to insist on, so it may be easier to simply visit each staff section and ask what recurring requirements they have of each company.

If your battalion *does* perform the required periodic inspections, then you should ask for a Subsequent Command Inspection Schedule. These are usually done individually by staff section and should be done every six months (but no less than annually). Include these on your battle rhythm, too, so that subordinates know when they should schedule staff assistance visits.

> Once upon a time, a new company commander visited his new boss for his initial counseling. As he stood at attention, he asked if the battalion commander had any guidance for him.
>
> 'Yeah! Don't f*** it up!' came the battalion commander's reply.
>
> After a short, awkward pause, the captain asked, 'Uh, could you be specific, sir?'
>
> 'I thought I pretty well was!' said the lieutenant colonel. 'Dismissed!'
>
> And that was the extent of the guidance for the afternoon.
>
> Guidance from higher doesn't usually come with as many details as we'd like. Nevertheless, your evaluation will hinge on how well you exercise disciplined initiative within your commander's intent.

---

[13] AR 1-201 §3-3c(2), 4 April 2008

Physical Readiness Training

Physical Readiness Training (PRT) is a commander's program, and as such it deserves just as much attention as any other program in your company.[14] You, as the primary training manager for the unit, are responsible for ensuring your soldiers are physically ready to support your unit's mission. Although first sergeants often take a personal interest in the quality of the unit's PRT, the commander's role is to assess, organize, direct, and sustain the overall physical readiness program.

First, you need to assess your unit's current PRT situation. Does the unit use FM 7-22 as its principal guide, and does it apply any relevant policy letters? Whether conducted by squad, platoon, or company as a whole, the schedule should be posted and each PRT session should look like this:

- A primary and assistant instructor brief the tasks, conditions, and standards for the day's PRT

- Warm up using the Preparation Drill

- Activities that are appropriate for the Army Force Generation (ARFORGEN) phase the unit is in[15]

- Cool down based on the Recovery Drill

- An After Action Review of the day's session

You should also look at your unit's PRT statistics. If PRT is executed by platoon, look to see if any one platoon leads or lags behind the others, and why. You should also check your MEDPROS profiles to see if there are any recent trends in injuries that would indicate areas that should change, and the unit's daily personnel statistics (PERSTATS) to see if there is anyone who is consistently absent.

---

[14] FM 7-22 §1-7, 26 October 2012
[15] FM 7-22 Tables 5-10 through 5-17, 26 October 2012

If PRT is not executed at the company level, circulate among the various platoons and squads. Ask questions of soldiers to see what they think about PRT. Do they like predictable repetition or variety? Do they work out at the gym in addition to PRT? Do they simply show up because it's their job, or do they have their own fitness goals?

Based on what you've assessed, you may want to organize things differently. Using FM 7-22 Figure 5-2 as a guide, develop the unit's policy letter for PRT. In it, be sure to include a stated purpose for the program. Is it:

- To prepare for a Joint Readiness Training Center (JRTC) rotation in the coming months?

- To help prepare junior enlisted soldiers for Warrior Leader Course and their duties as an NCO?

- To be the best in the brigade? (Be careful—commanders who establish higher standards should do so because their unit missions require soldiers to be more than minimally fit, and like-units should have similar standards.)[16]

- To achieve the highest APFT score average? (Again, another danger area—the APFT is simply one element of a total program, and should not be the foundation of your PRT program.)[17]

- To develop your soldiers' general health and fitness?

Establishing the purpose for your unit's PRT will help determine what kinds of activities your program planners should schedule.

"Soldiers should train to become stronger, faster, mobile, lethal, resilient, and smarter."—Frank A. Palkoksa, Director of the United States Army Physical Fitness School.

---

[16] AR 350-1 G-9d(2), 19 August 2014
[17] AR 350-1 G-9g(1), 19 August 2014

Having set the purpose and the policy, now assign responsibility for developing PRT plans to your first sergeant. In coordination with the Master Fitness Trainer (MFT), the first sergeant should submit drafts of the PRT schedule to you on either a monthly basis or as you submit your training schedules to battalion.[18] Compare the PRT calendar with the training calendar to check for conflicts; once approved, have it entered into DTMS.

The next task is to direct the various programs that fall outside the main plan for the unit. While installations usually handle the pregnancy/post-partum soldiers, what about APFT or body composition failures—how does your unit assist them? And what about temporary and permanent profiles? Are they grouped together or integrated with the rest of the unit? Your unit's Master Fitness Trainer should not be responsible for personally directing all these programs, but they should be available to teach NCOs how best to take care of their soldiers.

Finally, your job will be to sustain the system you've set up. This means consistently providing a leadership presence at PRT events. Don't be lured back to the office by something important—participation in PRT is one of the hallmarks of good leadership, and soldiers will definitely notice when you are not around. Plus, there are certain things you won't be able to address unless you are there.

Once you have your PRT program set up, the next level is to start integrating training tasks into the PRT schedule, effectively "killing two birds with one stone." PRT was never designed to be a standalone program, so make the most of every opportunity to handle multiple tasks at each event.

---

[18] AR 350-1 G-9d(1), 19 August 2014

Conclusion

As you can see, there is more to training management than simply scheduling required tasks—it's about being organized, knowing what needs to be done, and making the most of every training opportunity. As General Clarke's quote at the beginning of this chapter reminds us, we should not let non-essential tasks crowd out the essential ones. And in today's Army, where *so much* of what we do is considered essential, commanders have the challenging and difficult task of deciding which priorities get precedence over others.

BEST PRACTICES

"Until we can manage time, we can manage nothing else."—Peter Drucker

"People often complain about lack of time when the lack of direction is the real problem."—Zig Ziglar

If time management is important at a company level, it is even more important on a personal level. While it is true that commanders must have a good handle on their companies' day-to-day business, those who sit at their desks handling administrative tasks all day are not effectively leading their companies. Part of being "technically and tactically proficient" is minimizing the time spent on administrative overhead and focusing on what's really important. This chapter focuses on those best practices.

Managing Email

Most people begin their day by checking their email, but do so very inefficiently. Managing your email well will reduce the amount of "sand" that fills your day, making more room for the "big rocks" that really matter. Consider the following:[1]

---

[1] Adapted from "Best Practices for Outlook 2010," https://support.office.com/en-us/article/Best-practices-for-Outlook-2010-f90e5f69-8832-4d89-95b3-bfdf-76c82ef8

1. To increase the number of emails you can see, turn off the Auto-Preview and Reading Pane features. (View > Reading Pane > Off) These features may save you a click here and there, but reduce the total number of emails headers you can see in your Inbox. The more emails headers you can see, the better able you will be at distinguishing the *real* priority ones.

2. Don't "double-handle" your emails. As you read one, decide what to do with it—either respond to it, file it in a "Reference" folder, delegate/forward the task, or put it on your "To Do" list for the day. You will inevitably get all kinds of email from people who believe it's important to Carbon Copy (CC) the commander on their business; these you can delete.

3. Change unclear subject lines. We've all received "RE: (Unclassified)" emails from someone who forgot to enter something in a subject line. If the email's worth keeping, open the email and edit the subject line to something that makes sense.

4. Use a single folder (called "Reference") to save emails, rather than numerous folders for each topic. If you're concerned about finding the email later, you can mark it as unread (which will bold the header text) or search for it by sender, subject, or timeframe.

5. Limit the number of emails in your Inbox to one screen. You wouldn't use a paper inbox to hold all your files; similarly, your Outlook Inbox should have only those things which remain to be done—everything else should be filed or deleted.

6. Use a local ".pst" file to save space on the email server. If you've ever gotten a message saying your Inbox is full, or had people tell you they couldn't send you an email, contact your S-6 or the unit's information technology expert to create a local email storage file. Not everything should go there, though—store Serious Incident Report templates in an Inbox subfolder so that they can be accessed from any location via Web Mail[2].

[2] https://web.mail.mil/

7. Set up email signatures for frequently used email text (Tools > Options > Mail Format > Signatures). Ideal uses include welcome letters to incoming soldiers, reminders about upcoming mandatory training, and weekly reports. Your subordinates will also find this feature incredibly useful.

> *"Time management is really a misnomer. The challenge is not to manage time, but manage ourselves. The key is not to prioritize what's on your schedule, but to schedule your priorities."—Stephen Covey*

Managing Favorites

Web browsers can store your favorites, but it can be hard to keep track of the most important ones and stay organized. What if you had an entire webpage that clustered your favorites by subject in a two-dimensional layout?

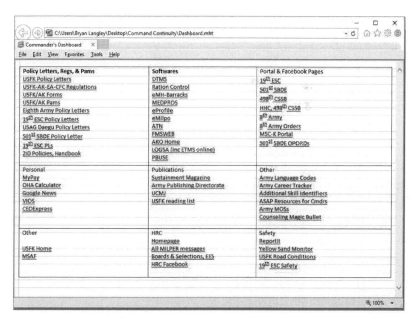

This was the idea for the homepage I developed as a company commander.[3] I built it to provide visual reminders of the sites I had to check on a regular basis, such as MEDPROS, eProfile, ration control, DTMS, ATN, eMH, ReportIt, my higher echelons' policy letters, and the Human Resources Command's evaluations site.

Even if local policy prevents using it as your homepage, it's still useful as a "one stop shop" of website links. You can develop it in Microsoft Word, save it on your desktop as an ".mht" file, and then save *that* file as a favorite.

> *"Don't mistake movement for achievement. It's easy to get faked out by being busy. The question is, 'Busy doing what?'"—Jim Rohn*

Managing Calendars

In addition to the training calendar, the company should maintain an administrative calendar to track tasks. This calendar, maintained by the personnel actions clerk (PAC), can be used to track the status of OERs/NCOERs, awards, personal records reviews, and DD93/SGLV updates.

Once the calendar is populated, the PAC can print out the weekly list of tasks (the "Weekly Agenda Style" works best) for your command team and platoon leadership, who can share it from there. This practice of providing visibility to junior NCOs can be particularly helpful in companies where platoons have only limited access to computers.

In small offices, the calendar can be shared among co-workers so that everyone has visibility on key events. This "group" calendar can be combined with personal calendars using the "View in Overlay Mode" feature.

---

[3] Based on the CEO Express website, www.ceoexpress.com

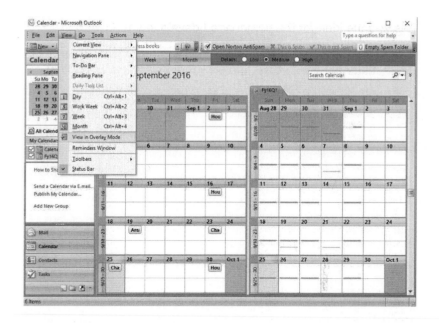

Administrative Meetings

Whether conducted once a week as a formal staff meeting or daily as an informal meeting with the first sergeant and platoon leadership, administrative meetings should cover the following:

1. Medical Readiness (including annual Personal Health Assessments, dental, and immunizations)
2. Scheduled maintenance services (including vehicles, weapons, and CBRN equipment)
3. Supply tasks (including lateral transfers/turn-ins, recons, equipment arrivals, cyclic inventories, and sub-hand receipt holder change-outs)
4. Upcoming events fit for SigActs and storyboards
5. Status on monthly reports (including the rating scheme, unit manning report, and unit commander's finance report)
6. Status on outstanding operations orders.
7. Status/feedback on NCOERs, awards, and quarterly counselings

8. Driver training schedules (and who will attend)

9. Barracks management tasks, including the fill rate, arrivals, departures, work orders, and eMH reports.

10. An additional duties review, to select replacements for soldiers departing within the next 90 days

11. A review of coin recommendations, promotions, and award presentations for the coming end-of-week closeout. (This is to give you time to prepare comments and check on preparations.)

12. Review of APFT and/or body composition failures.

13. Status of AR 350-1 training, if not covered in the training meetings.

When deciding whether to do large, formal meetings or informal, small groups, consider the nature of the topic. Driver training is hardly a sensitive matter, but the results of a monthly body composition weigh-in should be addressed in a more discreet setting.

"Time is the most valuable coin in your life. You and you alone determine how that coin will be spent. Be careful that you do not let other people spend it for you."—Carl Sandberg

How you adjudicate disciplinary action is up to you, but don't let a small minority of soldiers take up a significant amount of your time. Have your first sergeant prepare soldiers in advance so you can keep your UCMJ hearings quick and to the point.

File Management

The Army has promoted the digitization of paperwork for years (if not decades) and yet—amazingly—the number of signatures that commanders have to provide on a daily basis has hardly decreased. To maintain records on all the digital files you'll sign, you'll need a good file organization system.

As a company commander, I organized file folders by role: administrator, resource manager, coach, hammer, and training manager. Within each of those folders, I organized files by topic.

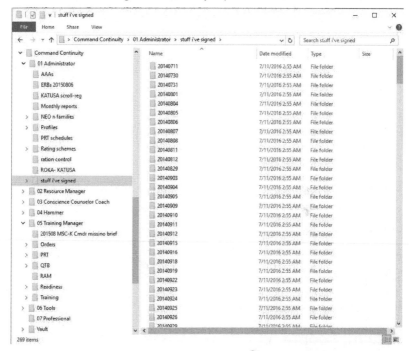

For each item I signed, I used a consistent naming convention. For example, a signed DA 31 leave form for PV2 Smith to begin on September 30th would be named **PV2 Smith DA31 20150930.** This way, if I had to go back and look for it, I knew what to look for. And if I needed to look for a DA Form 4187 to send someone as an example, I could simply look for "4187."

While most PDF forms can be kept in digital format only, there is one exception when keeping paper copies is important: inventories. Every month, file away the paper copies of updated shortage annexes and the working copies of both your sensitive item and monthly cyclic inventories. This way, no matter what happens to your computer, you always have something you can fall back on to rebuild your records.

Tracking Operations Orders

Your company is likely to receive far more operations orders than it can comfortably handle. To keep track of them all, develop a spreadsheet that tracks when they came in, what the task is, when it is due, who is responsible, and what type of order it is.

Orders can be described as one of four types, based on what their deadline: Single Instance, Periodically Recurring, Work until complete, or Not applicable. Even if something is not applicable, it's good to log it in case a FRAGO comes out later.

To keep track of the many operations orders your company will receive, designate a person in the company headquarters to log operations orders into a spreadsheet.

> *"Most of us spend too much time on what is urgent and not enough on what is important."—Stephen Covey*

Valuing People

Good management may help a unit run well, but units thrive when people feel valued. There should be more to being part of your company than simply showing up for work. Consider the following ways to show your soldiers that they are part of something bigger.

- *Barracks Dessert Night.* One night a month, use the barracks kitchen to bake simple desserts (like apple cobbler). Publicize the event through platoon leadership and ask FRG spouses if they'd be willing to help provide supplies.

- *Skills/Ambitions Database.* The Enlisted and Officer Record Briefs list Army information, but they do not capture hobbies, interests, or special skills. To better match soldiers with opportunities, build a binder of information you won't find in an Army database. As positions open up, try to place your soldiers where they can have the greatest impact.

- *Single Soldier Dinner.* These are best done during the holidays, when single soldiers are thinking about what they are missing out on back home. Dining facilities usually handle Thanksgiving well, but what about the other days? You can ask FRG spouses to put together a pot-luck and invite a guest speaker (such as the chaplain or a retired sergeant major) to speak to the group.

- *Training Montages.* Throughout the year, you will collect pictures for storyboards. If your unit will take part in a Christmas ball, assign someone to compile them in a video slide show to feature the unit's accomplishments. These pictures are also good to post in unit common areas so that soldiers can see their contributions throughout the year.

- *Birthday Cards.* It doesn't take long to write out a card for some-one's birthday, and it doesn't have to be eloquent, but the fact that you spent time thinking about the recipient is meaningful in itself. Even better, cite some of the person's accomplishments and thank them for being a part of the team.

- *Letters to Parents.* When first-term soldiers arrive, write a letter to their parents introducing yourself and talking about your values. Doing so is not only meaningful to parents, but a heads-up to soldiers that their life in the Army is not entirely separate from their family life.

- *Special PRT events.* Once a month, do something different for PRT. Go for an off-post run, do a hike, or host a family fun-run. My company was based in Camp Carroll, Korea, so we would hike up nearby Hill 303, the site of a POW massacre during the Korean War. Not only did it break up the regular schedule, but it gave soldiers a good perspective on the legacy of our service in Korea.

- *Good Conduct Medals.* The first (and perhaps the second) time a soldier receives a Good Conduct Medal, present it in a formation. (You'll find out if a soldier is eligible through the monthly reports.) If they've done their part in staying out of trouble, company leadership should do its part to recognize it.

- *Leader breakfasts.* Throughout each month, meet with different echelons of leadership to discuss issues that are important to them. One week might be junior NCOs, another week platoon sergeants, and a third week platoon leaders. It requires a thick skin, but it is the best way to learn about problems that won't ever be brought up through your Open Door policy.

- *Farewell luncheons.* As soldiers leave the unit, ask them about their experience and what you can do to improve soldiers' time with the unit. You'll learn much more from these soldiers (especially the specialists who are getting out) than you will anyone else, if only for the fact that they have no reason to fear any repercussions.

- *Invest in professional development tools.* Junior leaders often need help in developing writing, counseling, evaluation, and award skills. Build a small library where they can go to reference ideas.

Conclusion

Time management is less about managing time than being disciplined and efficient in performing your daily tasks. The less time you waste through inefficiency, the more time you can dedicate to the things that truly matter—the lives of the soldiers you serve as their company commander.

The following document for this chapter is available online:

1. Example Operations Order and Task tracker

View available documents at: asktop.net/mocc

Password: 88YEZX9

PREPARING FOR THE TRANSITION

> *"A great man leaves clean work behind him, and requires no sweeper up of the chips."*—Elizabeth Barrett Browning

What kind of legacy do you intend to leave behind when you finish company command? Will you try to prepare your successor for the road ahead, or leave them to figure things out for themselves? Do you intend to leave things better than you found them, or merely no worse than when you started?

Admittedly, the Army's evaluation system provides little incentive to ensuring a good transition. Nevertheless, how you finish your time in command will speak a great deal about your character, and in turn affect your professional reputation as an officer. So let's look at how to do it right.

Six Months Out

Twelve months as a company commander is the minimum to be branch qualified, but those who are serious about being considered for promotion to major should aim to complete 18 months. Whichever you choose, you should approach your battalion commander with a tentative timeline about six months before you intend to change out.

When deciding on a timeline, first consider how long it took you to complete your inventory. Did it take you the standard month, just two weeks, or did you have to file an extension? Look for a similar break in the S-3's long term calendar (plus a week, just in case) when there is no field exercise or major training activity to constrain the change of command inventory. When you have a date in mind, approach the battalion commander with your plan. You should also be prepared to discuss your "wish list" for your next assignment.

Over the next three months, develop the timeline and inventory schedules—not by date, but by day (Day 1, Day 2, etc.). If you've conducted your cyclic inventories to standard, refer back to your notes and to see how long each Line Item Number (LIN) or sub-hand receipt holder should take.

One more thing — successful company commanders typically receive the Meritorious Service Medal for their efforts. Because these require a general's approval, the initial submission date is usually 150 days before presentation, so this a good point to compile your accomplishments and provide a draft of your award to the S-1.

Three Months Out

At this point, follow up with the battalion commander to see if everything's on track for the date you chose. You should know who your successor will be so that you can make contact and go over the game plan with them. Three months will allow sufficient time to allow the new commander to attend the Company Commander/First Sergeant Course[1] and prepare for the transition.

To help the next commander prepare for the change of command inventory, send a copy of the property book (in Unit Asset Visibility Report format) and the Unit Identification Code (UIC). With these, the new commander will be able to get a feel for how the property book is organized, and

---

[1] AR 350-1 §3-39a(2), 19 August 2014

begin downloading manuals. Be sure to ask them about their schedule and when they expect to arrive at the unit.

At two months out, your supply sergeant should begin printing the BII and COEI listings for all the equipment on the property book (being sure to check on any technical manuals that have been updated). In addition, you should begin putting together your continuity book.

Your continuity book will be the next commander's greatest asset in their first 90 days, so be sure to fill it with the following useful items:

1. A memorandum welcoming the new commander to the unit
2. An in-processing checklist
3. A map of the installation
4. Links to any mandatory training the new commander must do
5. BN policies and where to find them
6. The point of contact for the Equal Opportunity representative (for the initial command climate survey)
7. Copies of the QTB and training calendars, with the command climate and initial command inspections scheduled
8. The point of contact at Army Community Services for the commander's in-brief
9. The weekly and monthly battle rhythms
10. A DVD of all the continuity files you've saved
11. The Pre-Change-of-Command inventory schedule
12. A copy of the AAA-162 personnel roster
13. MEDPROS reports (including profiles)

Six Weeks Out

The new commander should arrive at about the six week mark. After an orientation to the company's area of operations and a walkthrough of the different areas where property is located, the two of you should meet with the battalion commander to receive any specific instructions.[2]

[2] DA Pam 710-2-1 §9-3a(1)(a), 31 December 1997

Following an in-briefing from the property book officer, you're all set to begin the inventory.

At the end of each day's inventories, do a "hot wash" of what was looked at—the purpose is to make sure you're on the same page as the new commander. It will also help if the two of you are working from the same type of document, whether the property book is in the cyclic format, the PBIC format, or the unit asset visibility report. The goal is for the new commander to feel comfortable signing the property book, so be patient and don't rush the process.

While you're doing the change of command inventories, you should also begin integrating the new commander into the battle rhythm, and start giving them daily back-briefs on each day's events. If you have a QTB coming up, work with them on it rather than simply taking care of it yourself. You may think, "Well, I'm the commander until the day I'm not," but this perspective is short-sighted—your goal in your last month should be to smooth the transition, not push your own agenda.

Assuming you've followed the directions about cyclic inventories, any discrepancies in BII or COEI should be easily taken care of via the various relief of responsibility methods. If this is the case, your out-briefs to the battalion and brigade commanders should go very smoothly.

Change of Command Ceremony

You can draw up the invitations and the new commander may make the reservations, but the brigade commander's schedule is what determines the date for the change of command ceremony. Once they've blessed off on the transfer of the property book, they'll tell you when you may schedule it.

On the day of the event, you may receive your award in a separate ceremony, as well as a parting gift from your company. For the ceremony, your responsibility will be to schedule the location, design the invitations, and print them out (your orderly room can take care of this). You should also prepare a generous speech to thank your company for their support during your time in command.

The new commander's role will be to give you their biography for the pamphlets, schedule the reception luncheon, arrange for a cake, and provide refreshments (official funds may be available, depending on the unit). Custom dictates that their speech be shorter than yours.

Once the ceremony is finished and you've turned in whatever government phone you were assigned, the only thing left is to receive your evaluation, for which you will be told when to come in. If you've completed your command without the need for a Financial Liability Investigation of Property Loss (FLIPL), then congratulations! You've finished company command.

If not, well, let's talk about your FLIPL defense.

End of Command FLIPLs

There should be no surprises in your change of command inventory—any problems should have been identified beforehand, either in your cyclic inventories or in the pre-change of command inventory. Nevertheless, sometimes things happen and no one tells you—unserviceable containers get turned in for scrap, basic issue items get stolen, or computers get swapped out in a life-cycle turn-in. Unfortunately, for as long as you're the commander, you're still "responsible for everything [your] command does or fails to do."[3]

But that doesn't necessarily mean you're financially liable.

---

[3] AR 600-20 §2-1b, 6 November 2014

A FLIPL will be initiated on you if the dollar value of the loss exceeds one month of your base pay.[4] An officer will be appointed to investigate the circumstances within your company that led to the loss, and present their findings to the brigade commander to consider assessment of liability.

Yet before the investigating officer can recommend assessing liability, they must determine three things:

1. That there was a loss
2. That there was negligence or willful misconduct that violated a particular responsibility, and
3. That the negligence or willful misconduct was the proximate cause of the loss.[5]

In other words, it's not enough to simply show there was a loss—the investigating officer will have to show that you were negligent, and that it was *your* negligence that caused the loss.

These days, many units are under tremendous pressure to maintain a high mission tempo—so much so that events preclude them from properly accounting for equipment. Consider this email passage from one battalion commander:

> "Commanders, for now, I recommend you inventory all major end items identified on the cyclic list, select a shortage annex area to focus on as a commander during each cyclic (i.e., vehicle BII... or toolbox shortages, etc.), and delegate all remaining shortage annex looks for the remainder of the equipment to your company officer leadership. Two days max for you, perhaps a week for the company."

Essentially, this commander had directed that their subordinates ignore the requirement for all primary hand receipt holders to "inventory the required items with hand or sub-hand receipt holders" and

4 AR 735-5 Table 12-1, 10 May 2013
5 AR 735-5 §13-29, 10 May 2013

"make a visual check of the condition of the property."[6] The battalion's mission pace had become so demanding that conducting proper cyclic inventories was no longer feasible.

If you ever receive an email like this, immediately go out and get it framed—it will be essential in giving the investigating officer a full picture of conditions in your unit. It will also help in substantiating your answers to these questions:

- Did you receive the initial command inspection mentioned in Chapter Three? And an assessment of strengths and weaknesses upon completion?[7] If so, what weaknesses were identified in the supply section?

- Did you consistently have sufficient time following field exercises to perform a recovery?[8]

- Were you constrained (perhaps by the unit budget) from ordering necessary supplies, and what steps did you take to inform the battalion commander of these constraints?[9]

- Did you have sufficiently "qualified assistants"? If a supply sergeant position is filled with a 92Y supply specialist who has been reclassed, this could be a mitigating circumstance for the investigator to consider.[10]

- Did anyone else have responsibilities that conflicted with the supply sergeant's?

Ready answers to these questions will go a long way toward showing that while negligence may have led to a loss, but it wasn't your negligence.

---

6 DA Pam 710-2-1 §9-6b, 31 December 1997
7 AR 1-201 §3-3b, 4 April 2008
8 AR 710-2 Table 2-2h, 28 March 2008
9 AR 710-2 §1-9, 28 March 2008
10 AR 735-5 §13-29b(4), 10 May 2013

A battalion chemical NCO was under pressure from the brigade staff to turn in expiring medical supplies. Rather than involve the busy HHC supply sergeant, the NCO "exercised initiative" and turned in the supplies on his own, without a proper signature card. Although the NCO's action fixed the problem in the short term, it ended up creating more work for the HHC supply team and property book officer who then had to do "forensics" on the missing medications.

In another situation, one battalion S-6 shop had the common practice of swapping out user's computers without either recording the transaction on a DA Form 2062 or informing the company commander. As a result, the commander's pre-change of command inventory took weeks longer than expected.

HHC commanders must be sure to establish clear lanes of responsibility and SOPs for property exchanges. Failure to do so may result in statements of charges for equipment that is still in the unit's area of operations, but misplaced and unrecorded.

Conclusion

If the best route to establishing legacy in the Army is to help other people, it seems reasonable that the one person you should focus on helping the most would be your successor. The less time the next commander spends getting up to speed, the more time they will be able to spend helping others in the company.

EPILOGUE

"If, in the humility of our own errors, we can help others avoid the same mistakes, do we not have that obligation?"

As you've seen in the previous chapters, commanding a company requires as many management skills as leadership skills. There's a significant learning curve, but hopefully this book has helped fill in some of the blanks along the way.

As you look back on your company command time, you may find yourself thinking about things you could have done better or differently. This is normal, because the stuff you'd learned along the way is the result of the experience. Being in a leadership position has changed you – the responsibility has forced you to become the officer you are now.

With all luck, the things that you've learned from any mistakes you've made were not the result of professional ignorance. The purpose of this book has been to fill in the experience gap for company grade officers through best practices, examples, and lessons learned. Hopefully, it has made you a better, more competent commander, and the Army a more professional workplace.

THE
MENTOR

Everything You Need to Know About Leadership & Counseling

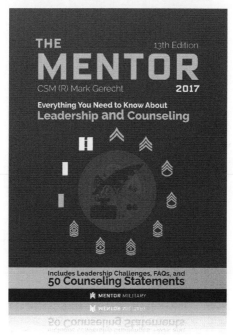

Includes:

- 50 Example Counseling Statements
- Guidance for Promotion Boards
- Tools for Preparing Young Leaders for Difficult Challenges
- Overview of Adverse Actions and Seperations
- And Much More!

The Mentor is the all-in-one leadership guide! It sets leaders and Soldiers up for success... and mentors them in the process...
—SFC Mac Arthur D. Ocampo

Find The Mentor and other great tools at MentorMilitary.com

Guidebook for the
YOUNG OFFICER

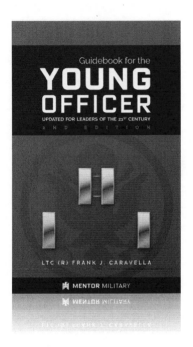

Guidebook for the Young Officer is LTC(R) Frank Caravella's little red book of Army Leadership secrets. Caravella guides junior leaders from their first days as officers in the United States Army up to battery or company command and beyond. How do you assimilate into your first unit? How do you determine your commander's expectations? How do you make a positive impact and steadily move through the ranks? The Guidebook provides thoughtful insight and proven principles that work. Reading this book is a great first step for any company grade officer who wants to improve his or her leadership potential.

I wish this book existed when I was a cadet and junior officer! Frank does a great job addressing most of the questions and situations that young officers face.
—Bronston Clough, former Army Officer and Ranger Instructor, and author of Get Tabbed

Find The Mentor and other great tools at MentorMilitary.com

Beans to Bullets
LOGISTICS
for Non-Logisticians

Make sure every leader in your unit understands Classes I, III, & V—your life and the lives of your Soldiers depend upon it!

- Stay lethal with **ammo & fuel** expertise.

  Water—turn your Achilles heel into an advantage.

- Improve morale with **quality chow**—it's easier than you think.

- Contains unique planning sheets for: Classes I & III that cannot be found anywhere else!

- Know the key players that make or break your combat effectiveness!

MENTOR MILITARY

Why Shop from **MentorMilitary.com?**

- Our product selection is curated **specifically for servicemembers**

- **Competitive pricing,** our prices are often lower than Amazon

- Most orders ship within 1 business day

- We ship to **APO/FPOs**

- We offer a 30-Day Money Back guarantee on our books

Visit MentorMilitary.com